The Skin of Meaning

Aaron Shurin

The Skin of Meaning

COLLECTED LITERARY ESSAYS AND TALKS

UNIVERSITY OF MICHIGAN PRESS

Ann Arbor

Published in the United States of America by the
University of Michigan Press
Printed and bound by CPI Group (UK) Ltd, Croydon, CR0 4YY

2019   2018   2017   2016   4   3   2   1

A CIP catalog record for this book is available from the British Library.

Names: Shurin, Aaron, 1947–
Title: The skin of meaning : collected literary essays and talks / Aaron
    Shurin.
Description: Ann Arbor : University of Michigan Press, 2016. | Series: Poets
    on poetry | Includes bibliographical references.
Identifiers: LCCN 2015033713| ISBN 9780472072965 (hardcover : acid-free
    paper) | ISBN 9780472052967 (pbk. : alk. paper) | ISBN 9780472121564
    (ebook)
Subjects: LCSH: Poetics. | Literature—Philosophy.
Classification: LCC PS3569.H86 A6 2016 | DDC 814/.54—dc23
LC record available at http://lccn.loc.gov/2015033713

Acknowledgments

Grateful acknowledgment is given to the editors, curators, and organizers who first supported this work in print and presentation (books and chapbooks, journals, anthologies, talks series, and symposiums) and who invited me into, or let me into, or couldn't keep me out of, the conversation, in which these essays were tested and shaped. The work appears almost entirely in its original form, to preserve a sense of the arc of history during which it was written. The site was and is San Francisco: gratitude always to that city of high light and lower chakras, which fosters the art of inquiry as an art of pleasure, and delivers its writers to hilltops . . .

"Like a Book" first appeared in *Tyuonyi*, number 6/7, 1990.

"Narrativity" was first given as a talk at the Painted Bride Gallery, Philadelphia, June 1989, and published as a chapbook by Sun & Moon Press in 1990.

"A Thing unto Myself" first appeared in *Code of Signals: Recent Writings in Poetics*, Michael Palmer, ed., North Atlantic Books, 1983.

"The Complexities of Measure" first appeared in *Interim*, volume 19, number 1&2, 2001.

"The Irruptive Text" first appeared in *Poetics Journal*, number 8, 1989. It is now part of the complete *Poetics Journal* Digital Archive from Wesleyan University Press.

"Noumenous *Men*" first appeared in *Poetry Flash,* June 1983.

"*Involuntary Lyrics*: A Foot Note" first appeared in *Involuntary Lyrics*, Omnidawn, 1999.

"Prosody Now" was first given as a talk at Poet's House, New York City, October 2012.

"Active Form: Towards a Gay/Lesbian Poetics" was first given as a talk for the Writers as Activists panel, Outwrite Conference, San Francisco, March 1990.

"Writing into the Twenty-First Century" was first given as a talk for the Writing into the Twenty-First Century symposium, Press Club, San Francisco, November 30, 1994.

"Queerly: AIDS and the Queer Imagination" was first given as a talk for the AIDS and the Queer Imagination panel of Queer Beats: A Symposium, San Francisco Art Institute, November 17, 1996.

"Lo How I Vanysshe: Afterword to *Codex*" first appeared in the chapbook *Codex*, Meow Press, 1997.

Unbound: A Book of AIDS was first published as a book by Sun & Moon Press, 1997.

"After Genet" first appeared in *Jimmy & Lucy's House of "k"*, number 7, 1986.

"Smoke" first appeared in the fourteenth San Francisco International lesbian and gay film festival guide, June 1990.

"Synching in Tongues" first appeared in the *Bay Area Reporter*, 1991.

"At the Pulling of Invisible Strings" first appeared in *Mirage*, 1985.

Contents

Preface

These writings and talks span more than thirty years, yet their concerns are surprisingly (to me, the lighthouse keeper) consistent: There's an affinity for the Romantic tradition in pursuit of a full-tilt writing I like to call "maximalism" — a lust to totally *possess* and *be possessed by* language; there's a fascination with the interplay of lyric and narrative components in poetry and prose; and there's a will to bust the code of the hidden, embedded power structures of — especially — gender and queerness, and release them back into the wild.

The spirit of the book is one of poetics, as *the* potent model for investigation, inquiry, and attention, just as the poem itself is the model for what is attended, the spinning center, a focus in tensile flux. The urge of such poetics is to peel back, dowse, scrutinize, and savor — and bow to the fire and bloom of meaning in multiple. Many of the pieces were written on request, for journals, panels, talk series and conferences; others simply grew to articulation under pressure of community conversations insisting on responses — led by the dynamic, restless, committed, poetry-besotted writing community of San Francisco and the Bay Area. Here one could believe that the life of poetry was/ is breathing and heaving like one's own, and that its life and health mattered exactly as lives do.

In the middle came AIDS, commandeering the life force and meaning alike. What else but poetics, with its devout Round-Table ardor, could meet the writing challenge, and travel to hell and back to make the heroes *heroes?* Elsewhere, in these pieces, heroism accrues to the poets themselves, from the masters of time, to the Master of Rhyme, from those just before — my teachers — to those in the 'hood — my co-conspirators — and those coming after — students and more — turning the turning pages . . . Gratitude to all of them forward and aft who keep me from complacency . . . and to that power in poetry which brought a sleepy boy into articulation, and dressed him for study, ecstasy, and battle all at once . . . and steadies his hand still . . . listening as he turns the turning pages . . .

I.

Like a Book

Having recently understood I was moving toward narrative in my writing — that moving being *narrativity* that interested me — to bring forward what I first called the Outside World, then Social Relations, and, finally, Evil, I'd felt compelled (a film documentary about the Lodz Ghetto in Poland helped break me down to it; an inhabitant had written in a secret journal, "If anyone got out of here alive and had the chance to blow up the whole world, he would do it — and he would be *right*." The moral assurance of that statement seemed to me as far upside down as one could go, horror, ruined, forsaken, living in total pain — hell's literalness — the blackest thing I think I ever heard said) to read Holocaust writing, and found myself on summer vacation picking up a copy of Primo Levi's *Survival in Auschwitz*. I saw my timing, and thought to open the book when I returned, thereby not sabotaging my release time on Cape Cod. But one is commanded by books as much as the other way around, and so in bright June open early summer in Provincetown I found myself entering Auschwitz, trying to survive. The tides that rise and run from the small bay leave slick and shiny mudflats in the late afternoon, the dusty light brings things to serene paleness, washed away, withdrawn hushed isolated pilings, and form the sweetest of moments in P'town whose picket-fenced sweetness is sometimes too neat, cloying. The long sand-cliffed Truro beaches of Longnook and Ballston are the archetype of heat-blasted summer delirium and luscious nothingness. *Survival in Auschwitz*, there, and *Survival in Auschwitz* on the white chenille bedspread by lamplight, and in the peony garden on white wrought iron. The book read like a book; I read it like a book, turned pages toward their narrative projections, relished perversity and antagonism as well as heroics (survival) — that's narrative tension — and shuddered at my inability to find a deeper, more problematized way in. Is it not writing but *reading* that's in trouble post-Holocaust? What model of reading would properly hold for such an encounter? Would I have to stand thigh-deep in ice water, read by penlight in an airless closet? Or would the writing itself need to change reading, would it need to discomfit, to use dream's technique of fracture and surprise, paranoia's looming enlargements, hunger's hallucinations, pain's throbbing rhythms, identity's multiple (dis) locations, politics' layered lies (all of which are possible functions of referentiality and narrativity, suitably fucked up) to break the habits of reading formed by studious information gathering and pleasure? To make these uneasy arrivals alluring enough to encounter — the way Dante makes you willing to go through Hell — is a compelling challenge I'm being given, dangerously.

[1990]

Narrativity

I'm interested in the utilization of both poetic and narrative tensions: the flagrant surfaces of lyric, the sweet dream of storied events, the terror of ellipsis, the audacity of dislocation, the irreversible solidity of the past tense, the incarnate lure of pronouns, the refractability of pronouns, the simultaneity of times, the weights and balances of sentences. I'm interested in lyric's authenticity of demonstration and narrative's drama of integration; lyric, whose operation is display, and narrative, whose method is seduction. I describe a set of binary terms across which I see writing passing an exchange of values, and it becomes a multiple texture/text — writing in just those created tensions between surface vocalic tangibility and referential transparency; between theme and emptiness, measure and interruption, the eternal present and past of memory/future of dream; all present, all heightened, operational. Such conflated writing would be worthy of Barthes's definition of the text: "not a coexistence of meanings but a passage, an overcrossing; thus it answers not to an interpretation, even a liberal one, but to an explosion, a dissemination."[1] One seeks to be out of order, to shiver out of subjectivity, to shake off the mask of the material *and* to shimmy in its arms, to finally retreat from logic and advance by radial maneuvers, gathering meaning. "To break the sentence," says Rachel Blau DuPlessis — and here the sentence carries its overtone of imprisonment without parole —

> rejects not grammar especially, but rhythm, pace, flow, expression: the structuring of the female voice by the male voice, female tone and manner by male expectations, female writing by male emphasis, female writing by existing conventions of gender — in short, any way in which dominant structures shape muted ones.[2]

One looks for alternate methods to proceed, to use and subvert the codes at hand: stanza, line break, character, plot, point of view.

In "The New Sentence," Ron Silliman suggests ways in which the prose poem has used combined and measured sentences to interiorize poetic structure, foregrounding language operations and surface values in a writing mode — prose — whose usual form is the syllogism, building structures of projection and depth. "The torquing which is normally triggered by linebreaks," he points out, "the function of which is to enhance ambiguity and polysemy, has now moved into the grammar of the sentence."[3] The paragraph as a unit of quantity and the sentence as a unit of measure, altered sentence structure, controlled and limited integration: these devices begin to conflate the values of poetry with those of prose. Other writers have pursued not just prose but narrative prose, and foregrounded narrative codes to awaken a reader's attention to process as well as result. In his novel *Jack the Modernist*, Robert Glück uses metaphorical and metonymic litanies side by side, showing off the writing as writing as he demonstrates that the devices are not mutually exclusive.

> I grab his cock, unpromising, and he says in mock bewilderment, "What's that?" As it hardens I answer for him, "It's my appendicitis, my inchworm, my slug, my yardstick, my viola da gamba, my World Trade Center, my banana, my statutory rape, my late string quartet, my garden god, my minaret, my magnum opus, my datebook, my hornet, my Giacometti, my *West Side Story*, my lance, my cannon, my nose-job, my hot dog, my little sparrow, my worm on the sidewalk after a storm, my candle, my Bic, my unicorn, my drawbridge, my white whale . . ."[4]

and on for another sixty substitutions, "my cyclops . . . my *Venus of Willendorf* . . . my Dark Tower." Four pages later the elaborative metonymic process of prose takes over from the comparative metaphorical process of poetry.

> My troubles were too numerous to consider all at once, their sheer quantity defeated me. My mom would say, "Write a list, get a handle on your problems, deprive them of their active

ingredient, time." So I found a clean page in my yellow legal tablet . . . Nuclear catastrophe, destitution, famine, additives, melanomas, losing face, U.S. involvement in El Salvador and Nicaragua, Puerto Rico, South Korea, Chile, Lebanon and Argentina, war in the Middle East, genocide of Guatemalan Indians and extermination of the native peoples of Brazil, Philippines, Australia, answering the telephone . . . toxic waste, snipers, wrinkles, cult murderers, my car . . .[5]

Though these are both descriptive processes, they are not transparent; the reader is aware of being in a list, enjoys the ingenuity of elaboration and substitution, is held to the surface of the writing at the same time she is integrating the lists into the larger structures of the story. Speaking of description, Alexander Gelley writes,

> This kind of stillness in the narrative may be likened to islands of repose for the reader, moments of collection. The hold that the level of plot, speech, and action exercises on him is loosened. His attention may wander, but it may also adjust to a changed mode of apprehension. I am suggesting that the more circumstantial the description and the more separate from the narrative in which it is embedded, the greater will be the reader's part, and the more he will be forced to assume a stance for which the narrative proper offers little support. . . . When the familiar codes of narrative are blocked or diverted, reading/writing becomes problematic, and the subject of/in the narrative shifts from the characters or the author to the reader. . . .[6]

This problematization forces the reader to ask questions, to become active in the role of reader, and Glück reinforces this tendency by confronting the reader directly in his stories, "You'll understand my fear," he says, "because television has trained us to understand the fear of a running man;" and, "I can only give this story, which is the same as sitting with my back to you;" and, "Tell me, given the options, where would your anger have taken you — where has it taken you?" By confronting the reader, Glück not only breaks the window of his narrative but creates and engages an audience, creates a social registration for his writing by direct address, by luring the "real" time of the reader into the "dream" time of his story. The foregrounding of devices and codes does not neutralize them, they are too full of historical determination, but it can ritualize them, or expose their ritualization; reveal them not as necessities but constructions — open to change.

Writing might use narrativity without succumbing to its hegemonic orders of linear development, unity of time/tense — and apart from the modernist reconstructing modes of memory and dream. A prose whose paragraphic groupings themselves might be based on measure, whose higher integrations might be thematic or associational rather than developmental. "How tenacious is our happiness!" says Kevin Killian in *Shy*. "Unlike narrative, it invents and eludes itself from moment to moment; it lacks conventions; its shape has no outline, its formal properties those of the cloud — numinous, portentous, hungry. . . ."[7] And then goes on to produce a narrative with properties of the cloud, numinous and hungry, where characters search for themselves alongside the writer as a character himself, where persons encounter each other but never stoop so low as to engage in a plot.

The ceiling was gray and smooth as the beach that Gunther Fielder lived by. Flat, and peaceful, the way that "now" is without a past or future to rock it up any. He could focus on the gray and try to hypnotize himself, closer towards death. "Do it," he demanded.

"My name is Harry Van," he said. It sounded so false. He said it over and over, didn't ring true somehow. Like somebody else who you couldn't remember. Well try again, something new.

"I'm David Bowie," he said, experimenting. "I have come to earth a space invader, hot tramp, I love you so." Oh that was so suffragette, trying to "be" a star.

He'd start again. "Hi, my name is Mark the dead boy," he said with great difficulty.

Yes.

"Are you Kevin Killian," he replied. "Can I help you?" Just like the Hot Line!

These voices came out of his mouth from nowhere, between heaven and earth, this conversation developing like a photograph pulled from its tray full of crystal chemicals. Emergent.[8]

These voices attack the proposition that characters or author must be unified presences, and suggest that self itself may not be locatable along such a monochromatic line. He is telling you now a story about narrativity, he is telling her story. She finds the story as she looks at each other: so many faces. She is crossing gender from the start, she wants you to know she is Elizabeth Taylor — and has the Halloween photos to prove it. He is a boy playing Puck in a high school production of *A Midsummer Night's Dream* wearing ballet slippers forever. "I have died and am in a novel and was a lyric poet, certainly, who attracted crowds to mountaintops."[9] I come after Robert Duncan but before Norma Cole. My name is "Broiling-Days-In-A-Little-Patch-Of-Shade." "For better or worse," says Flaubert,

> it is a delicious thing to write, to be no longer yourself but to move in an entire universe of your own creating. Today, for instance, as man and woman, both lover and mistress, I rode in a forest on an autumn afternoon under the yellow leaves, and I was also the horses, the leaves, the wind, the words my people uttered, even the red sun that made them almost close their love-drowned eyes.[10]

"Voice," "Person," "Point of View" — always singular — propose a unified filter through which events may be organized, and, as filters screen properties, screen out toxins and tannins and pieces too big to fit neatly. But pluralities are possible. "I see only from one point of view," says Lacan, "but in my existence I am looked at from all sides."[11] Pronouns are known as shifters because they are by nature unstable linguistic units, referring not to people but to moving circumstances of speech and audition, visibility and perception. As such they are fictional *opportunities*; unlike names they permit a character to be subject and object, to ride the Wheel of Person, speak and be spoken of with equal weight, inhabit simultaneity. Here is a poem from Alice Notley's sequence, "Congratulating Wedge":

No I wouldn't know why anyone would
want to write like that. I should never
have had to do it. We were used to this
other thing we always know like when we're
here. And you have this clear head & you're
seeing things & there they are. You don't
notice they're spelled. That's how you
know you're alive. I never saw you
looking like a dictionary definition & if I
did I wouldn't tell *nobody*. People
aren't like that. They say, Hey
asshole motherfucker turn that radio
off! *But the sun's playing on it!* But
it ain't real, you dumb package!
I recognize every package the way it
comes. Now I'm mixed up. But I
always wanted to be a package, person
thinks. Do they? Or, I gotta define this package, me. Or, God if only
I was a package but I'm not.[12]

What *are* people like and what method correctly presents/
represents them; from what angles are they constructed and
who construes the angles into voice? In her mind as "I," out of
her mind as "she," confronting or confronted by "you"; conspir-
atorially social and partial as "we"; part of one another, occasionally indistinct, certainly indiscreet, we are and we are not separate people. "My premise, in general and in writing," says Leslie
Scalapino, "is that I do not think there is a man, or woman, or
society, social construction; though it is there. It is not there."[13] I
have been marginalized as a poet, homosexual, counterculture
protester, drug taker, transvestite and Jew; I am as interested in
boundaries for what lies outside them as in. I would like to drop
my "characters" onto the sharpened point of a gemstone, so that
the radial fractures would illuminate a comprehensive pluralis-
tic image.

Syntax is the plot of the sentence, a systematic ordering of
person and event, of who does what to whom and when and to
what end. Encoded in its structure are a variety of fixed agree-
ments that always end in a point (.) Who will speak for beside-

the-point? Nouns and verbs must have parallel numbers, pronouns and verbs parallel persons; tenses must agree to produce time that resembles progression. Business conveniences that make of stories little prisons of discrete power relations with seemingly invisible walls. I am not talking about referentiality vs. non-referentiality; I'm talking about how narrative referentiality might be better served. Gender is foregrounded and elementalized, digressions are trivialized, passive constructions frowned upon. As Sarah Schulman points out, try to tell a lesbian story without names: she came into a room, she looked at her, she looked at her, she said — and *aside* from homophobia, what terrors would such unlocations unleash? Normative pronoun usage subjects self *and* other to power/dominance models of unity and authority, of he over she and it beneath them. For pure syntax there is Charley Shively's reduction of the phallocentric rule: "the subject fucks the object."[14]

Here is Leslie Scalapino writing:

> The young person living there, having an intense tortured as if tearing in half pain in the middle, waking lying asleep, though this had only occurred this one time. The day and night being free of the one person, who hadn't had this tortured sharp pain as if to tear her in half except this one time, the man lying waking staying gently with her during it through the soft darkness and then ending in the warm balmy day with the people around who go down the street.[15]

Passive participial constructions which don't inhabit time, genderless and then confusing gender assignations, unlocated relative pronouns, erratic time shifts without one simple present tense: an amalgam of person and event that keeps elements suspended and active, "an explosion, a dissemination" of meaning. "His mouth are everywhere," I wrote erotically in "Honor Roll," insisting that the plural verb was truer to the polyvalence of desire.

And I have neither a coherent story to tell nor can I cop a coherent attitude to give my voice a characteristic singularity. I was born in sleep and raised in sleep and wake up to find myself sleepwalking. The figures I know all have shadows; some figures are smaller than their shadows. In the first photo I am a soft blasted thing, mouth open tongue hanging, blotto. Six weeks premature, I was still "in here" out there. The *world* was unformed, coalescent. His story is the story of an intuited world, a story where digressions may be the point, where ellipsis is an accurate representation of what there is.

This world in its order decomposes into air, simultaneously present and absent. A writing, then, of enmeshed simultaneities, which gives sufficient weight to its constituent presences so that they verge upon each other. The material relations of the Unknown. "The stuff of the psyche," says Herakleitos, "is a smoke-like substance of finest particles, that give rise to all other things. . . . it is constantly in motion: only movement can know movement."[16] His story pulls the reader down from the surface of language not to rest but to ride back and forth between the manifest and imaginary worlds, among selves. "I wanted to write a story," he begins, "to talk about the outside world and escape my projections, but the outside world could not escape from my projections. I wanted to write not 'my' story but 'theirs'; I wanted to write about evil." He looks at his fingers to escape your accusations; a sunbeam deconstructs him into motes. He is happy dissolved there, and wants to write from such dissolutions, melting into the grain of his lover's nipples. He has no lover; he has entered an argument about narrative and political ruination. "Tell me your story," he asks, and you do.

Here in this dialogue writing relies less on information, as Walter Benjamin shows, than on the moral power of interpretation, "to keep a story free from explanation." It is left up to the reader to "interpret things the way he understands them, and thus narrative achieves an amplitude that information lacks."[17] Here a fabricated house open to the wind is both a shelter and a sharpener of the wind's bite, a house of shadows and a moving shadow that resembles a house. *Narrativity*, the action not the thing, a happening semblance that is and is not a story, a gift given and taken away so that one must finally stand fulfilled by transgression. Narrativity, a process of integration not linear but aggregate, circular, partial — and so, complete.

[1989]

Notes

1. Roland Barthes, *Image — Music — Text*, Hill and Wang, 1977, p. 159.

2. Rachel Blau DuPlessis, *Writing beyond the Ending*, Indiana University Press, 1985, p. 32.

3. Ron Silliman, "The New Sentence," *Talks, Hills* 6/7, 1980, p. 214.

4. Robert Glück, *Jack The Modernist*, Gay Presses of New York, 1985, p. 27.

5. Ibid., p.32.

6. Alexander Gelley, *Narrative Crossings*, Johns Hopkins University Press, 1987, p. 14.

7. Kevin Killian, *Shy*, Crossing Press, 1989, p. 103.

8. Ibid., p. 161.

9. Michael Palmer, *Sun*, North Point Press, 1989, p. 83.

10. Gustave Flaubert, *The Letters of Gustave Flaubert, 1830–1857*, Belknap Press of Harvard University Press, 1979, p. 203.

11. Gelley, *Narrative Crossings*, p. 27.

12. Alice Notley, *Margaret & Dusty*, Coffee House Press, 1985, p. 68.

13. Leslie Scalapino, in correspondence, 1989.

14. Charley Shively, *The Advocate*, #342, May 13, 1982, p. 24.

15. Leslie Scalapino, *The Return of Painting*, unpublished manuscript.

16. Herakleitos, *Herakleitos and Diogenes*, trans. Guy Davenport, Grey Fox Press, 1976, p. 18.

17. Walter Benjamin, *Illuminations*, Schocken Books, 1969, p. 89.

A Thing unto Myself

The unRomantic Self and Gender
in the Third Person

I am in a pronominal funk, where the crisis of subjectivity in which the so-called Romantic self is under attack crosses purposes with the tyranny of gender located in the third person, giving my many selves consternation and causing a panic in their vocabulary. This crisis in subjectivity, already articulated in the later Nineteenth Century, challenges monolithic and static conceptions of self in favor of a multifaceted or liquid identity, and the resulting psychological and cosmological restructuring dovetails with contemporary challenges to authority itself, questioning who has the right to speak for whom? Where and how does one gain authority to speak in the midst of contrary and varying social forces constituting identity, a socio-linguistic milieu where the pronouns known as "shifters" may be accused of shifting the blame as well as shifting the responsibility? As linguists reduce the province of "I" to a narrower and narrower present moment of discourse, a vast amount of the matter of self gets rerouted to the status of third person, the exclusive domain — in English — of gender, so that the liberation of person, of consciousness in the form of "person," is threatened at its second remove.

Rimbaud's 1871 letter to Izambard is famous for its pronouncement "I is an other," fracturing the complacency of first-person discourse. Earlier in the letter he states, "It's wrong to say: 'I think'. One must say: one thinks me."[1] Here the use of the third person is direct in combating authorial majesty — the "I" is reflexive, and has no right to its creative presumption. Though the I/Thou relationship has a long history in poetry in the form of the poet directly addressing her soul, his heart, her self (thus becoming firmly entrenched in the discourse of person), Rimbaud projects the self into the realm of what Emile Benveniste calls the non- or third person, whose indication is not presence but absence. With this distancing Rimbaud adds the what-I-am-not to the what-I-am, enlarging the possibilities of discourse.

And before Rimbaud, or contemporaneous with him, both Emily Dickinson and Walt Whitman began to offer similar possibilities toward an expanded image of self. Though it might seem, at first, that Whitman was propounding — especially in his grandiose "Song of Myself " — one huge monolithic self, he was actually careful throughout to locate multiple points of reference for this large identity — "Walt Whitman . . . a kosmos," yes, but though "I am large, I contain multitudes." In this multitudinous self are many simultaneous voices, not just Whitman's: "It is you talking just as much as myself, I act as the tongue of you" and "Through me many long dumb voices." The multifaceted self grows directly out of Whitman's concept of democracy as a mass of individuals, and, in fact, by the later editions of *Leaves of Grass* he had chosen to open the volume with a short poem in which the original "Myself" was now put in the frame of the third person: "One's-Self I sing," he begins, "a simple separate person, / Yet utter the word Democratic, the word En-masse."[2] So far is he now from insisting that kosmos be labeled with his particular name that he merely refers to himself as "one" among a larger one that is actually a many, a "masse."

In a poem questioning her own sanity, Emily Dickinson points to a multiple self as source of the trouble, and she does so with a seeming awareness of the first person's exclusive location in the "present" moment of discourse so that a past "I" is actually a third person. ("*I* can only be identified by the instance of discourse that contains it and by that alone. It has no value except in the instance in which it is produced." — Benveniste[3]) "And Something's odd – within –" says Dickinson, "That person that I was – / And this One – do not feel the same – ." Though there may, indeed, be an emotional or psychological root for the severing of her integrated sense of self, she is adamant in her poetry about giving this self its multiple locations, whether she is referring to a "dead" self ("A Breathing Woman / Yesterday") or a living counterpart that has actually acquired its own name

("We don't cry – Tim and I, / . . . Then we hide our brave face / Deep in our hand / . . . I – "Tim" – and Me!")[4] I will talk more of this pronominal switch, but notice, here, how she has taken the "I" and located part of it squarely in a third person, in "Tim." Benveniste and Roland Barthes offer linguistic analyses for this narrowing realm of unquestioned first-person authority. "*I*" can be used only in the present, and can refer only to the person speaking: "*I* is 'the individual who utters the present instance of discourse containing the linguistic instance of *I*.'" (Benveniste) This is the only way to gain the authority necessary to make one's self the subject: "It is by identifying himself as a unique person pronouncing *I* that each speaker sets himself up in turn as the 'subject.'" The shifting nature of the first person trades this authority back and forth in discourse or writing/reading between the I and Thou, for, as Barthes notes, "The *I* of the one who writes *I* is not the same as the *I* which is read by *thou*."[5] According to Benveniste, the third person, because it (she/he) exists outside of this immediate discourse involving subjectivity, is actually not in the realm of person:

> There are utterances in discourse that escape the condition of person in spite of their individual nature; that is they refer not to themselves but to an 'objective' situation. This is the domain that we call the 'third person.'
>
> . . .
>
> As has long been seen, forms like *he, him, that,* etc. only serve as abbreviated substitutes (Pierre is sick; he has a 'fever'); they replace or relay one or another of the material elements of the utterance . . . the 'third person' is indeed literally a 'non-person.'

Any word that thus takes over for the authorial subject other than "I" is in this area of non-person, a first person that is a "thing" unto itself. A dislocation or multiplication of the autonomous self thus projects objectivity into the zone of subjectivity, offering an assault on conventional linguistic foundations:

Language is possible only because each speaker sets himself up as a *subject* by referring to himself as *I* in his discourse. Because of this, *I* posits another person, the one who, being, as he is, completely exterior to me, becomes my echo to whom I say you and who says *you* to me. (Benveniste)

The multiple self who is reflexive, who is both subject and object in her own discourse, brings *relation* into language in a new way, brings relativity forward as simultaneous perspectives on the event of discourse — the immediate constitution of identity speaking for the world.

Ron Silliman, in his introductory essay in *Ironwood 20* to an anthology of new "realist" writers, points to an un-located or discontinuous "I" as a primary characteristic of the group of writers he's discussing. (Though there are certainly others who share this particular methodology.) Silliman notes:

These writers do not simply sing of the self. Instead, these works investigate its construction through the medium of language. . . . We do not contain multitudes so much as we are the consequence of a multitude of conflicting and overdetermined social forces, brought to us, and acted out within us, as language.[6]

Thus Silliman brings social and political reality squarely into relation with the matter of identity and subjectivity in discourse, pointing not only toward multiple locations of identity but multiple constitutive forces that are themselves creative of identity.

"But to whom might such an art communicate directly?" he goes on to ask. "Self-reflexivity (i.e. a conscious response to alienation) is clearly a requirement." It would be necessary, he adds, to locate "those individuals for whom this question of the subject of self is neither abstract nor peripheral, but is as real and concrete (and problematic!) as everyday life itself." I've suggested that the deconstruction of self brings the "objective" third or non-person into the subjective realm (or vice versa). It is also clear that the domain of this third person, in its singular form in English, is governed by the House of Gender, that place of fierce behavioral definition, modification, and reward. It will be necessary, then, to look with a cautious eye toward the role of gender in the third person as a constitutive force for identity, and to look toward those people for whom gender is already at issue in their everyday lives as just "those individuals" Silliman is seeking for whom the issue of self is concretely problematic.

The force of gender in determining identity in our society can hardly be overestimated — it is constitutive at every conceivable level of social interaction, going far beyond a merely physiological foundation into areas of behavior where physiological gender is irrelevant. Yet its distinctive binary terms continue to enforce themselves. At significant levels gender is projected onto the self as primary identity itself, before personality or individuality. The awareness of one's place (or misplace) on the axis of gender puts the third-person objective into the realm of the first-person subjective. "They came in with rags and a belt," says Bertha Harris in *Lover*, describing the event of her first menstruation. "They said, Now you are a woman. *I* had been exchanged for a woman."[7]

Similarly, men whose supposedly "girlish" ways throw their gender categorization into some confusion — and these ways may fall among a number of behavioral patterns from speech to walk to position in intercourse — have primary, though "confused," gender identities projected onto them, defining them. In explaining her difficulties with gender tyranny over her identity, Gayle Rubin draws upon both Sartre's analysis of racism and anti-Semitism — where the Jew's subjective sense is destroyed by others' sense of him as an object, an "other" — and his analysis of Genet's homosexuality, his "situation as the object which he is to others over the subject he is to himself . . . The fact that Genet is first an object indicates the origin of his particular brand of sexuality."[8] (Some contemporary historians such as Weeks and Altman are beginning to describe the historical process by which homosexual "acts" came to be seen as constituting a homosexual "identity," creating object-status.)

"Beyond that," says Bob Glück in *Elements of a Coffee Service*,

a certain word was growing in me, a word too charged for the newspapers, for books, TV, even for my father's jokes. When I located Homosexual under H in the index of library psychology books, the sight of it jarred me, my stomach clenched—blushing, I averted my eyes. It went way beyond fuck, shit, or piss; in its clinical remoteness it went beyond nigger, dago, spick, kike; it would grow and become large as I was, equaling me. If the word was so despised, what would become of me once I had given it corporeal form?[9]

The confusion is dramatically linguistic; the attempt to locate self along an axis of power, or access to power, forces the readings: I is she-that-is-a-woman or I is he-that-is-not-quite-a-man. At the merest level of reportage, gender signification has an overbearing and potentially warping power — as any homosexual writer knows who has had to brave, or cow to, social opprobrium against same-sex love. The switching of pronouns to fit social erotic convention is powerfully indicative of both an awareness of the tyranny of gender and the mutability of identity. It is in this context, that both Whitman and Dickinson switched erotically charged pronouns, and we have, luckily, both versions of these poems.

Whitman's famous "Once I Pass'd through a Populous City," placed among his "Children of Adam" poems that describe so-called amative heterosexual occasions, tells of a liaison with an unknown woman in an unnamed town. For years this poem was pointed to as proof of Whitman's supposed relationship with a woman in New Orleans, who was also supposed to have given birth to some or one of his children. "Yet now of all that city," says Whitman,

> I remember only a woman I casually met there who detain'd
>   me for love of me
> Day by day and night by night we were together — all else
>   has long been forgotten by me,
> I remember I say only that woman who passionately clung to
>   me,
> Again she holds me by the hand, I must not go,
> I see her close beside me with silent lips sad and tremulous.

Some sixty years after the initial publication of this poem it was revealed that, in the original manuscript, the erotic import was entirely different. "But now of all that city," Whitman wrote, "I remember only the man who wandered with me, there, for love of me," adding, "I remember, I say, only one rude and ignorant man who, when I departed, long and long held me by the hand, with silent lip, sad and tremulous." Such manipulation of gender and its pronouns is enormously suggestive of Whitman's ability — we might call it necessity — to find multiple locations and multiple voices for the self.

Dickinson employed the strategy of cross-gender terminology in several poems and letters. I've already mentioned the pseudonymous "Tim," and Rebecca Patterson reminds us in her study *The Riddle of Emily Dickinson* that "Emily, too, liked to pretend that she was a boy. In her letters she sometimes spoke of her 'boyhood' and in many poems she was 'boy,' 'prince,' 'earl,' or 'duke.'"[10]

The poem beginning "I showed her heights she never saw" is crucial to Dickinson's work, depicting a moment that recurs — symbolically amplified and metaphorically turned — throughout the poems. This moment is charged with romantic and erotic weight, fraught with psychological intensity, and sundered in its moment of glory by a deep refusal. "Would'st have me for a Guest?" asks Emily, but "She could not find her Yes – / And then, I brake my life –." This passionate poem, directed to a woman friend, was nevertheless rewritten in later years so that it read, "He showed me heights I never saw," etc. We also have two versions of the poem beginning variously, "Going to Him! Happy letter!" and "Going – to – Her! / Happy – Letter!" In this dialogue between the writer and her letter, filled with emotion directed toward its receiver, Emily not only switches the entire set of pronouns in the two versions, but refers to herself in the third person: "Tell Her – just how she sealed – you." Dickinson's articulated junctures resonate here with a deeply kaleidoscopic sense of identity. "Tell Her," she says to the letter, "I only said – the Syntax – / And left the Verb and the Pronoun – out!" Whether from fear or insight or parts of both, Dickinson cracked through the rigidity of gender-located pronouns in pursuing the articulation of her self and her desires.

I mean to suggest that those for whom gender signification is seriously at issue might be inclined toward manipulating pronouns, and since they are not fixed for themselves they need not be fixed for others. There is a rich field of homosexual subcultural parlance exploring cross-gender identity, and an equally fierce attack by contemporary women on formerly sacrosanct territory of the male pronoun. To expand the area of the objectified-as-woman woman, women have begun to explore the associative cultural identity of males, enlarging their sense of self toward its fuller possibilities. Judy Grahn's "She Who" poems offer a litany of such exploration:

> She Who continues.
> She Who has a being
> named She Who is a being
> named She Who carries her own name.
> . . .
> I am the woman the woman
> the woman – I am the first person.
> and the first person is She Who is the first person to
> She Who is the first person to no other. There is no
> other first person.[11]

Similarly, contemporary women — and in fact many gay men — have resurrected the term "goddess" in describing their spiritual potentialities, not so much to replace one binary term with another, but to explode gender signification in the highest of all the third-person powers, otherwise known as "Him."

No group, I think, has been more inventive — and again this may be the invention of necessity — in exploding traditional gender terminologies than gay men. It has been an age-old custom of gay men to replace their masculine-signifying first name with feminine ones: John becomes June, Louie becomes Lulu, Mark — Marcia, Ron — Veronica, David turns to Vidra, Aaron to Irene, and for decades there has been the all-purpose "Mary." Or perhaps a little dramatic characteristic or dream of power will locate itself behind the introductory "Miss": Miss Bigfoot or Miss Anaconda or Miss Ecstasy. (In the true spirit of non–gender specificity, a friend of mine — buoyed by the very articulated personality of his dog — has opted not merely for Ms but for Mx, thus being non–species specific as well.) There is a long line of simple "girls," as well as girline, girlfriend, girlfrenzia, and

21

girlthing. And behind these, in a kind of majestic purity, waits the absolute pronoun itself: "She," filled with cultural determinism, fraught with psychological fundamentalism, resonant of mythology. The powers that are projected or transferred *onto* the female are thus transferable making cross-gender terminology akin to sympathetic magic. And here I would profess my own opinion that though there is certainly misogyny among many gay men, this freedom with feminine pronouns and gender-identified words is not meant to be demeaning to women — it is meant to demean the system of role signification that distributes moral, intellectual, and social characteristics along gender-specific lines. It is used to crack presumptions of behavior and privilege, and to redistribute the goods. In much the same way women seek to gain for themselves territory formerly reserved for males, many gay men seek access to territory previously circumscribed for females. Both of their experiences are born from role objectification (as well as sexual objectification) so that the self becomes a thing to others and ultimately a thing to itself. Thus, Miss Thing is the grand ironic nomenclature in gay terminology — the perfect person-as-object!

Actually any objectified quality projected as a state of identity will serve as well; witness Genet's account of the evolution and declensions of the "Quite":

> "No," said Mimosa, "I'm the Quite Alone."
> She also meant: "I'm the Quite-Persecuted."
> . . .
> "My God, I'm the Quite-Giddy!"
> . . .
> "I really am, sure sure sure, the Quite-Profligate."
> . . .
> "Here, here, behold the Quite Fluff-Fluff."
> One of them, when questioned by a detective on the
>   boulevard:
> "Who are You?"
> "I'm a Thrilling Thing."
> Then, little by little, they understood each other by saying:
>   "I'm the Quite-
> Quite," and finally: "I'm the Q'Q'."[12]

The pronouns of gender are tyrannical. Because they exemplify the social, cultural, and economic factors embedded in gender-role modification of behavior, they animate the supposedly non-personal realm of the third person with their own constitutive energies. I would suggest, then, that gender signification distributes person onto the axis of the non-person, substituting cultural gender determinism for identity. Explorations toward a reflexively expanded self must not be caught out in this trap. There is a vast territory for analysis and discovery in both gender signification and the mutability of pronouns. A world of multi-subjectivity and multi-objectivity waits somewhere.

[1983]

Notes

1. Arthur Rimbaud, *Complete Works and Selected Letters*, University of Chicago Press, 1966, p. 302.

2. Walt Whitman, *Leaves of Grass, Comprehensive Reader's Edition*, Norton, 1965; "Song of Myself," "One's-Self I Sing," "Once I Pass'd Through a Populous City," and in Gay Wilson Allen, *The Solitary Singer*, Grove Press, 1955, p. 252.

3. Emile Benveniste, *Problems in General Linguistics*, University of Miami Press, 1971, pp. 218, 220, 221, 225.

4. Emily Dickinson, *The Complete Poems of Emily Dickinson*, Little, Brown; "The first Day's Night had come –," "I've dropped my Brain–My Soul is numb –," "We don't cry – Tim and I,," "I showed her Heights she never saw –," "Going to Him! Happy Letter!".

5. Roland Barthes, *The Structuralist Controversy*, Johns Hopkins University Press, 1972, p. 141.

6. Ron Silliman, *Ironwood* 20, Vol. 10, No. 2, 1982, p. 65.

7. Bertha Harris, *Lover*, Daughters, 1972, p. 102.

8. Gayle Rubin, *Masculine/Feminine*, Harper Colophon, 1969, p. 238.

9. Robert Glück, *Elements of a Coffee Service*, Four Seasons Foundation, 1982, p. 79.

10. Rebecca Patterson, *The Riddle of Emily Dickinson*, Houghton Mifflin, 1951, p. 129ff.

11. Judy Grahn, *The Work of a Common Woman*, St. Martin's Press, 1978, p. 78.

12. Jean Genet, *Our Lady of the Flowers*, Grove Press, 1963, p. 121ff.

The Complexities of Measure

Who I want to be or think I am in fancy; how the world should make justice shine; the revelatory power of what (I think) you ought to know. Oh I'm a stupid fuck, why trust me? My bitter revenges equal my noble sentiments; my cheap sentimentality crowds my scrupulous invention. All I wanted to say — *all I thought to give you*— is contradictory, speculative, moment. Standing on this shifting ground (San Francisco fault lines) requires the precision of attention I'm calling today the complexities of measure.

Grandiloquence makes sense to me most times I look at the sky so I'm not afraid of Romantic gestures. [I'll do things in writing I wouldn't *wear*, that's for sure — and I probably wouldn't wear the sky — though I did just buy a midnight blue tunic with azure panels that I thought neatly acceptable but my boyfriend sweetly struggled to damn with faint praise.] I mean language leads me into places I'd otherwise fear to go. Yesterday a student listed for me all the things he hated to do in writing. That's his lesson for next week, of course. What revelation is he afraid of? May I undercut you please? Disjunction, interference, multifoliation: my senses proper.

If I knew myself well I probably wouldn't write, but I'm a sleeper. I'm drawn to writing poetry to keep me awake. What sins I'd otherwise try to get away with! This way all I have to do is *see* them. Who's out there? The baby's eyes lock: "Now I'm making sense of the world!" I'm not a model of action, I'm not of princely behavior, but I know what sweet song is, and I can rock you to sleep with it, I'm a sleeper. But the sweet song is also the morning lark's: wake up! Contradiction is the synchronic view of a dialectic.

What the poem permits me to make is the meaning I'm after. There's a precision of attention that clarifies relations, and when the phonemes slide I'm in heaven.

[2001]

The Irruptive Text

"Come with me": that would be a proper beginning, as if the writing (reading) were not just a journey through time but through space as well, an actual site, site-specific. Across the pages an extended landscape unfolds to the wandering eye, "before our eyes." Writers know it first — the white desert of the blank page — and readers follow the map inscribed.

Safe within the luxury and quirk of my reading habits, I meet the Victorian adventure novelist H. Rider Haggard, the great geographer. In the squarely referential dimensions of his prose, an old romance transpires: the excitement of *place*. We have our new romances of presence and solidity — *echt*, the text itself! — but how comforting, still, the sign in working order can be, a hand on your shoulder, a hand to cup yourself into, a body to lean on and a place to stand. To lean *through* writing onto the conjured elemental landscapes of Africa (*She, King Solomon's Mines, Nada the Lily*), Asia (*The Return of She*), Oceania (*When the World Shook*), Iceland (*Eric Brighteyes*). The plots of these novels are shadows of each other — lost civilization found by chance ruled by ageless queen, Rousseauesque fantasies of primal nature hatched in the industrial age and fleshed out by the bloody artifacts of colonial imperialism. What fascinates is that along the way the way itself rises up, claims the compositional energy. *Where things happen*: a hard flirtation in a shrinking and increasingly perceptual world with one of the powers of the art.

In Haggard, landscape is the agent of the plot, purely external points of resistance which the heroes encounter and by which and through which they are moved toward their destinies.

If your Way is the life you are living to reach, each place here is a thing in the way; not just a marker but a site of compositional resistance and release. Here is a mountain, you must find it; here is a mountain, you must climb it; here is a river, you must ford it; here is a marsh, you must cross it; here is a volcano, you must encounter its heat.

The table of contents will read like a map: (5) Our March into the Desert; (6) Water! Water!; (7) Solomon's Road; (8) We Enter Kukuanaland. And maps themselves appear as sketches for the action, the proposition:

> I, Jose da Silvestra, who am now dying of hunger in the little cave where no snow is, on the north side of the nipple of the southernmost of the two mountains I have named Sheba's Breasts, write this in the year 1590 with a cleft bone upon a remnant of my raiment, my blood being the ink[1]

and produces a map whose plot runs across the Kulukawe River, along the Forty Leagues, up and over Sheba's Breasts, and down Solomon's Road to the Mouth of Treasure Cave. How can you get there from here.

Haggard's mock-heroic prose is notoriously stiff and clunky, his characters merely types, but when he situates them his writing opens up. The climaxes of his novels take place in the wildest imagined scenes, dwarfing the characters, swallowing the action. It's the fire movies stole from the novel: panorama, landscape as setting and as set (implying action: the rock *behind which*), the beauty and thrill-terror of the "natural" world, an autonomous force which rises up to meet you, the way colliding tectonic plates push down into each other and rise up to form a mountain. The irruptive text. This is not a sacred terrain — though the books are shot through with spiritual yearning — but a defiantly external one, by which a "man" might still be measured — and sustaining within it the contradictions of domination and loss, of simultaneously dominating the world and being lost in it.

The world rises up to meet you: how perilous, how safe! One's adventure is bound by these tangible particularities. In one chapter (23) of *She* you are taken out of a secret cave, across the plain surrounded by cliffs (the whole thing an ancient empty lake bed), to the ruins of old city walls surrounded by a moat, through the temple ruins four acres wide, up a flight of broken steps to a chamber hollowed in a stone wall, back around the palace ruins into the inner shrine of the temple. Next chapter, back through the city across the moat across the plain to the foot of a rock wall that forms the lip of a volcano, rising up two thousand sheer feet. Don't stop; up the slope to a kind of ledge that leads into a crevice along a path, winding inward "like the petal of a flower," to a cave, and twenty minutes deep into the narrowing cave, creeping.

> Before us was a mighty chasm in the black rock, jagged and torn and splintered through it in a far past age by some awful convulsion of Nature, as though it had been cleft by stroke upon stroke of the lightning. This chasm was bounded by a precipice on the hither, and presumably, though we could not see it, on the farther side also . . . It was impossible to make out much of its outline, or how far it ran, for the simple reason that the point where we were standing was so far from the upper surface of the cliff, at least fifteen hundred or two thousand feet above . . . The mouth of the cavern that we had been following gave onto a most curious and tremendous spur of rock, which jutted out in midair into the gulf before us . . .
> "Here must we pass," said Ayesha.[2]

That done, you climb into the heart of the nearly extinct volcano, a rock chamber into which slices, at intervals, a spear of flame that carries the secret force of life.

Anything that transpired here would be potent; the place itself is an inspired event. We have labored to get here but exhaustion is matched by awe. For nothing is as tangible as rock, even that touched through the trick of fictional signification. The confirmation is that of the existence of the Other; solid, formidable, *there*. *The* world (ours) is replaced by *a* world; here by elsewhere. Yes, "asleep" in the armchair, wrapped in the genius of the passive reading experience, the seated person to whom things happen, the person who is "taken" somewhere else. Erotic, submissive, physical: Take me (away). One of the dreams of fiction — to walk through the door of the word out into the world.

II.

I want those rivers and mountain walls — ah, those *words* of rivers and *words* of mountain walls. Unlike our shifting territory of displacement and disjuncture — present on the surface but lost down below — the romance of the referent promises a loss at least grounded in the body, "Take me anywhere, anywhere; / I walk into you, / Doge — Venice —"[3] Determined, I put my feet in the text. I don't have rivers and mountains. I take *his* rivers and mountains. I put them here.

Collage, erasure implosions, subversions: recombinant methodologies by which texts encounter other texts and mutate. We pose the instability of the sign but the solidity of the signifier; the mutability of history but the integrity of the text. In our exile among the contentious simulacra of meaning, the text *stands for* the real, a historical unity. We are at home in the text, in place, grounded here. I read in our writings that encounter other writings (and write them) a yearning for context, not de-context, and find there the pleasures of site and scape — the shapes of creative resistance reminiscent of the old adventure. Another language of rivers and mountain walls.

I have, for the old, Homer's *Iliad*, Book XXI, in which the river Scamander rises up from its bed to encounter Achilles on his bloody march toward Troy. The river is not merely a place in the way; it's an intercessional force, a landscape still possessed of elemental deific power. But through its currents the gods rouse to meet Achilles in material guise, shaping his struggle as a story line, a man trying to cross a river.

> . . . but the river rushed upon him with surging flood, and roused all his streams tumultuously, and swept along the many dead that lay thick within his bed . . . In terrible wise about Achilles towered the tumultuous wave, and the stream as it beat upon his shield thrust him backward . . . Howbeit the great god ceased not, but rushed upon him with dark-crested wave, that he might stay goodly Achilles from his labour, and ward off ruin from the Trojans.[4]

And take for the new David Melnick's *Men in Aida*, a homophonic transliteration into American vernacular of Homer's literal Greek.[5] The place of resistance and formation is text against text. The sounds of the *Iliad* itself rise up to meet Melnick, shaping his (our) lines, rolling over him in their waves. At all times this "wall" of sound bounds *Men in Aida*, impinging upon its urgencies, keeping its phonemes in line. Certainly any formal proposition contains or directs a work's flow — the way banks direct a river — but here the guiding principle is an actual *site*, on the bookshelf, by me on the desk, and *referred* to. The two places make simultaneous incursions — irruptive — producing a new interactive locale. "Be, dare. Up Atreides Agamemnon a tone deck kick on in."

There are various strategies for such encounters. Erasure: Ron Johnson's *Radi os*, where *Paradise Lost* stays in place as a new writing forms from it, out of it, the original submerged — ocean bottom — from which islands of the new arise.[6] *Paradise Lost is there* among *Radi os*, one and the other. Johnson's "signifier" is pulled away from its object, but the act of reference is still dynamic: reference *and* rupture. Or Claude Royet-Journoud's poetry which composes and decomposes itself along an elaborate route of intertextual self-influence. Original texts — perhaps hundreds of pages — are first written in prose whose sole purpose is to generate further writings and disappear, so that after several stages the final poems have genealogical traces — sedimentary — to the original language-as-event. The poems are locked, compositionally, into a complex chiaroscuro which includes both intention and result; writings shadowed by more and more previous texts, earlier and earlier forms of themselves — like Notre Dame rising on its forgotten pagan altar.[7]

So we find in texts themselves a solidity, a context. If we take this previously "used" language, are we released from the burden of signification while we reproduce its terms, find ourselves grounded elsewhere while we are set free here? We locate history in literature and pose ourselves against it in a frictional interrogative stance. As in Michael Palmer's *Sun* (the long version), a 434-line parallel (the same length) to *The Waste Land*, which imagines itself as a response to Eliot — question, not answer — investigating tacit assumptions of signification and naming, decrying cultural bombast and hegemony while it yearns for culture and tradition, situated as it is in a hothouse of "literary" discourse, deriving its terms from supermarket tabloids (*Sun*), Lewis Carroll, Eliot, and recrudescences of Palmer's own work in progress.

Write this. We have begun to have bodies, a now here and a now gone, a past long ago and one still to come.

Let go of me for I have died and am in a novel and was a lyric poet, certainly, who attracted crowds to mountaintops.

For a nickel I will appear from this box. For a dollar I will have text with you and answer three questions.[8]

I wanted those mountains and rivers so I took them. In *Elsewhere*[9] I have used Rider Haggard's language of landscape — *my* dream of content — to produce/reproduce a significant territory, incurred upon and deranged according to my experience. His dramatic locales (and the stories they propose), imploded and conjoined, shape my own text with their shadows, their seeming referential solidities and their actual linguistic forms. I do not know the story — how could I, I'm writing it? I imagine a physical world in which I can walk disembodied, a compassionate tale filled with actual horrors, a gigantic mountain shaped like the word "mountain," and a volcanic core where the fire of life blazes because I say so — and by which I am consumed.

[1989]

Notes

1. H. Rider Haggard, *King Solomon's Mines*, Octopus Books Limited; reprint, 1979, p. 25.
2. H. Rider Haggard, *She*, Octopus Books Limited; reprint, 1979, p. 387.
3. H.D., *Hermetic Definitions*, New Directions, 1972, p. 4.
4. Homer, *The Iliad*, Harvard University Press, 1951, pp. 425–427.
5. David Melnick, from "Men in Aida" in *Boundary 2*, vol. XIV, no. 2, Fall 1985/Winter 1986, p. 43. Melnick's poem takes the sounds of Homer's words and finds in them English words that have the same sounds.

6. Ronald Johnson, *Radi os*, Sand Dollar, 1977. Johnson takes an edition of "Paradise Lost" and actually erases parts of the text; the words that remain form a new poem: "*Radi os.*"

7. Claude Royet-Journoud, see *Une Methode descriptive*, Le Collet de Buffle, 1986; and, trans. Michael Davidson, "A Descriptive Method" in *Temblor*, no 7, 1988.

8. Michael Palmer, "Sun," in *O One/An Anthology*, ed. Leslie Scalapino, O Books, 1988, p. 178.

9. Aaron Shurin, *Elsewhere*, Acts Books, 1988. The language in *Elsewhere* is collaged entirely from the novels of Haggard.

Noumenous *Men*

On David Melnick's Men in Aida

A text resounds with intimacies local to its writer, generic to the language, peculiar to the reader. But what if a text takes on not just its own but another language, and another text as well? That's *Men in Aida*, a homophonic transliteration that literally *re-sounds* Homer's *Iliad*. The Greek phonemes dislocate and reform themselves into their English counterparts, so that — given a certain leeway — both the *Iliad* and *Men in Aida* run their course concurrently. It's a case of shadow text with an aggressive twist: Homer's Greek is a syntactically fluid construction with little juncture; Melnick's English is full of juncture and monosyllables that highlight the isolationist pull of consonants. When *Men in Aida* is read fast so as to override its junctures, the English (American) falls away and the Greek comes forward.

You come on us, Danaans, sit thee up, rope your son, a fine ace ass.

Don't fall away, that's just the setup, the poem is high velocity and set to its own funky taps. What's formal literary/rhetorical in Homer becomes colloquial and street smart in Melnick. Two tensions warp the poem to its own giddy pace. The pressure of tailing the Greek forces super-syntactical surprises that enliven the English. In fact, the snaky Greek syntax brings out a fluidity in logical old English — Melnick's phrases touch their toes and scratch their backs while containing, nevertheless, a syntactic order. And since Melnick at all times is led by the ear, a melismatic high play enlivens the language. A goofball rapture pushes through the literary construct to give it chant power; it's got the heat of rap pacing its reconvening phonemes.

Pale lay days decks out he's a tart tear eyes a' pacin'.
. . .
Comin' on cat at you, moan, you zone. Hi ya goon, ache us.

Somebody's pulling from underneath, language and more. (*a hue / In undy*). Like an id shadowing an ego, the Homereros makes its way through the poem. Maybe it's the id of the Achaians whose names float up (*Human men theoi doyen Olympia dome attic on teas*) among their American buddies, a nice cross-cultural grope, with the immortals' names untranslated to lend the eros a little dignity (*Hera, Teddy, Poseidon, Guy, Pallas Athena*). It's a gay epic, gay because that word's paratactic insistence becomes a *theme* of the poem, and because Melnick's own hungry erotic beat-up but upbeat longings drive the language.

Ache I on a rope alone, guy guard on a wreck, day oh say sting.
. . .
Ach, so alone! Ode aching echo lows. A tie on Kenny come I.

True to Homer, Melnick is commandeered by Aphrodite, taken on *her* ride like Paris and Helen, called into her presence. In the *Iliad*, Hera solicits the aid of Aphrodite so she may temporarily divert Zeus. Aphrodite reaches into the folds of her *peplos* and comes out with an untranslatable *thing*, a belt or thong, elaborately embroidered with scenes or signs. That *thing* is her *it*, the seed-power of her creative eros. It's got desire, will, and against-your-will worked through it. When Zeus and Hera lie down under its sway, the earth immediately blooms into hyacinths and crocuses. Put that power to language and you've got the undertow of *Men in Aida*. Sometimes Whitmanesque (*A moan, lick, oh sandy ocean. / All if I'm me, merit*), sometimes ecstatic (*Jesu! Pee! Lay (day), pant on neck, aglow. That tanned Ron!*). If he's in her service, maybe the poem can service him:

Muse sound I Aida. Nah, may bummin' I hope eke a lay.
. . .
Ach! Noumenous men.

The formalist proposition of *Men in Aida* highlights the range of congruities possible in language. When are we not pursued by another, shadow, mirror, precursor, friend, or foe? Melnick's taking on his Homeric transliteration is a blow at monotheism and hideous duality alike. A gem of consciousness through which facets dream of their kinfolk radiance. A play of forces by which one thing always stands for something else. What other epic announces itself in this same dance of phonemes?

[1983]

Note

David Melnick, *Men in Aida, Book One,* Tuumba Press, 1983.

Involuntary Lyrics
A Foot Note

The line is dead; long live the line!
After fifteen years of prose poems I was wondering a way back
to verse. The End of the Line I had envisioned — surfeit of the
Projective's obsession with lineation — started reviving. I was
missing a torque one feels in the body of thought.
Orders are delivered: Each "Involuntary Lyric" ends its lines
with the same words as a corresponding Shakespeare sonnet —
though these rhyme-words have been shuffled out of sequence
to spring their traps (to *unring* the sonnet.) With these moored
but mutated determinants the lines turn on a hinge (sometimes
there's just the hinge), projective only in the sense of being shot
toward Shakespeare's word already waiting there. A new measure is unloosed — vertiginous but restrained — within these
fixations.
Poetic constraints quicken me, foils to my florid sensibility and voluptuary lexicon. An art like S&M, perhaps [which
isn't my art of eros], where boundaries pressure the interior
that cooks. Vanilla S&M? — maybe, since there's plenty of play
against the rigor here, with swinging indeterminate line-lengths,
and wide-open topical windows.
Windows privilege the daily; I wanted "involuntary" to include
what experience was doing to me. Composure unrobes: hilarity
or severity. The quotidian acts as a given, just as Shakespeare's
language is given to the poem. Not to be coy (Elizabethan as it
may be) but it makes *attention* my mistress (OK, he's in drag).
Ballasted by the end-words poem to poem, the *Lyrics* fuse incursions from the left hand to the fixed but floating stations of the
right. Alternating modes high or low, meditative or notational,

they attempt to balance what's being given: the measure of attention. The *tension* of attention.

If divination is suggested, one is raised by language as one raises it. Theme? Age is in my hand I find, and love-called-desire rouses its own cognitive prosody. They play on me, poor fool or master, poor Puck, little cup of mortality. I couldn't announce a theme to which I didn't become subject.

I was happy to invite back in to my poems names and places [hello, friends] and let my own contradictions find their voices. Though I didn't *read* the *Sonnets* for *Involuntary Lyrics* — their semantic weight being much too powerful and me far too suggestible — interplay was inevitable: didn't erotics bleed right through, with so much incidence of direct address and all those cruisy "eyes"? Still, I've relished contemporary circumstance among the strictures and structures, so the Renaissance's "little death" happens vertical in a park as well as the romantic boudoir. Doubling syntax, popping rhyme and fine unfashionable abstractions are similarly evoked, scions to the shameless exuberant Elizabethan vocabulary or shadows of its rhetoric.

If I've been fearless in maneuvering this territory it's because Shakespeare's *Sonnets* are in the tradition so fundamental as to be almost transparent, merged with their process and moment, which are elementary, elemental. They're primal material, almost as pure as the flowering language itself — in this case, I might say, as pure as Form.

[1999]

Note

Aaron Shurin, *Involuntary Lyrics*, Omnidawn, 2005.

Prosody Now

This is a talk with four beginnings.

For the first we are deep in moonlight, though it is purely textual light, since we are indoors, in the hallway of a Spanish-style house in Los Angeles circa 1965. In that verbal shimmer and glow I've flung myself across the carpeted floor to perform for my mother and brother the soliloquy that will be my tryout piece for *A Midsummer Night's Dream*, our high school senior play. I am deliriously inside the spell of the spell-casting sonorities, as Oberon prepares Puck to begin his mission of mischief. "I know a bank . . ." he instructs and I declaimed, drunk on iambs and perfume, "I know a bank where the wild thyme blows, where oxlips and the nodding violet grows quite overcanopied with luscious woodbine, with sweet musk roses and with eglantine. There sleeps Titania sometime of the night, lulled in these flowers with dances and delight . . ."[1] The hallway carpet was a bed of flowers in which I too lay down in moonlight and drowsed . . . In the end, you may have read elsewhere, I was chosen to play not Oberon but Puck — nu, look at this face, who else? — but having voiced and memorized and rehearsed the Oberon lines, I held them close inside me — shall I call this somatic prosody? — for over thirty years, cherished and foundational . . . right up to the point that I began to teach a course in Prosody for the graduate writing program at the University of San Francisco.

The week's topic was "The Line," and in particular the metrical line, with further inflections to come via Pound, Williams, and Projective Verse. By luck or magic I happened to be walking through Golden Gate Park — *that* flower-strewn bank — and chanced upon the Shakespeare Garden, which I'd passed many times before but never yet entered. There I found, among the living representative plants, the *textual* flora as Shakespeare had named them, engraved as quotations on a stone wall. And there — of course I immediately searched — I found the coordinates of my beloved forest glade, where Oberon avowed, I read, "I know a bank *whereon* the wild thyme blows . . ." Excuse me? Whereon? *That's* a mistake! Should be, as I'd memorized long ago, "I know a bank *where* the wild thyme blows," not "whereon the wild thyme blows." Did I have it wrong all these years, was that possible, did I have a somatic prosody malady? I ran home to Google — perhaps then it was Alta Vista — and found there was some scholarly contention as to whether the line should have scanned as perfect iambs — meaning some scribe had dropped the *on* in *whereon* — a position adhered to by a number of conservative noodle-heads, including our Golden Gate protectors of regularity in verse — or whether Shakespeare had intended the broken foot, enacting a small caesura inside the iambic swoon. This is my first beginning. What is prosody? It is not just the difference between noodle-headed regulators and actual poets; it's the study of, or the attention paid to, the shifts of meaning in the shifts of balance in the tiny pause of a syllable suspended as a breeze blows or a petal falls. It is the possibility of "where" against the probability of "whereon."

For the second beginning let me take you to my apartment in San Francisco circa 1981, where a group of poets and enthusiasts have gathered together to form the now somewhat-famous Homer Club — an informal spinoff from the Poetics Program at New College of California — with the lunatic aim of acquiring ancient Greek and reading the whole of the *Iliad* in the original simultaneously. Many of us knew not a word of Greek, but we had passion for poetic study, and, not incidentally, the ferocious appetite of group captain Robert Duncan to motivate us. And so, foolishly, doggedly, triumphantly, I clopped my way through dictionaries and the crib of multiple translations — aided, I'll say, by a Motown-inflected natural ear for rhythm — to mark the rise and fall and rise of the Homeric hexameters as they roused the troops and swung the sails and heaved the bloody spears on the fields before Troy. We chanted together to hear the aural imprint of the oral epic, in our California accents and tone-deaf attempts at pitch, and we felt the beat of the mythical poet's staff as it tapped out the points of the six flexible feet. *Menin aiede thea, peleiados achilleos . . . Dum-de-de dum-de-de dum dum dum-de-de dum-de-de dum dum.* I would learn to call these units dactyls and spondees, but before that I would lie awake for hours with the sonic hoofprints of the beat galloping through my head . . . *not* the Greek words, which I'd instantly memorized and recited, but the pure hexameters, *before* language, *before* the poem. What is prosody? It is the performance of humility before the great powers of form-in-language. It is the name of the galloping horse tearing through the fields of a restless dawn on its essential mission to gather poetic meaning. It is, as *The New Princeton Encyclopedia of Poetry and Poetics* has it, "meaning given figured and textured shape."[2]

And that is the third beginning. It nests among the 1,400 pages of the dense and weighty tome affectionately known to those of us who dragged it to class each week as The Doorstop. A giant scholarly work, this poetry encyclopedia, filled with chronologies and exacting historical details, reams of secondhand theory, a postmodern predilection for defining things in multiple versions as "some think that . . ." and "others say that . . . ," and a cover-to-cover inebriation with terminology, often obscure, occasionally obscurantist, sometimes acute, and, I've long suspected, frequently cooked up on the spot in vats of neologisms, attended by mad linguists and lexicographers, to pierce the hearts of readers and fill the encyclopedia pages regularly with fresh blood — the way I've always imagined the secret ingredient of my grandmother's hand-grated potato pancakes to be just a drop of knuckle blood.

And yet as an inveterate neologizer — and one who laps up developmental chronologies of art — I've regularly used the *Princeton* as the text in my Prosody course. For that it has offered me "semantic density" to describe the way poetry uses elements of form to achieve multiple concurrent layers of meaning; it has given me the similar, ungainly, yet fascinating, "plurisignation" to describe the way that layering sustains ambiguity and keeps meaning in flux. What is Prosody? It is, says the *Princeton*, in its best combination of polysyllables-for-the-love-of-polysyllables and analytical lucidity, the study of "those extensions, compressions, and intensifications of meaning" made possible by an increase in formal structures, including elements "phonological, morphological, syntactic and perhaps discursive," in processes "metrical, sonal, rhymic and stanzaic."[3]

Rest assured, I don't take this terminological influx lying down — even stretched out in wild thyme and woodbine — and "sonal" and "rhymic" make me delirious. I have another lexical swoon, but take the challenge. If there is a poly excess of syllables here, what might we call it? Syllabicity, of course. If the syntax overwhelms, what is that? It's syntaxation. The elements and powers of form we call prosodic are those we can name and describe, and so students completing my course in Prosody have received a Certificate of Achievement from the Stanzaversity of San Francisco, for their mistress/mastery over, to name a few, iambiguity, metaphormulation, enjambmentarianism, concretinism, hyphenomena, verse-atility, and imargination.

New forms demand new terms, that's clear, as the sonnet is replaced by the Fibonacci series, and the broken foot recast as erasure. And new or old the elements of form transform themselves: bronze armor and fairy-king capes alike drop away to reveal the hidden skin of meaning. Structures and figures that seem, initially, to be non-semantic — those iambs, enjambments, hyphens and margins, methodologies and constraints mentioned above — *become* semantic in the transactional site of the poem, where — (*whereon*) — everything signifies.

If the poem layers its elements toward a dense simultaneity, prosody separates the layers in order to glimpse the dynamics at play in the whole body of the whole art. For the last beginning, or the fourth layer, we tumble back to that white stucco house, to a time well before the nodding violets, or at least to when they were merely buds, a purple swell. In the budding thick of adolescence, I sit on my bed; open before me is a weighty volume — the original doorstop? — pulled from our newly gifted set of

40

the *Encyclopaedia Britannica,* noble in its wine-colored naugahyde boards and O Britannia pedigree, authenticated by the shocking spelling that joins the *a* and *e* in *paedia* in an act of English swagger, a scholastic throwdown. I am poring over illustrations of the human body — is it volume A for "anatomy"? — (paying special attention, of course, to the reproductive system) — rapt by the revelations of the unseen forces at work inside of me. In this deluxe edition the fine illustrations are printed on acetate transparencies, in a series of overlapping layers that foreground, one by one, page by page, the skin, the musculature, the nerves, the circulatory system, the skeleton, etc. From the initial page the body can be seen as a structure of many simultaneous forms. It has semantic density. As the leaf-after-leaf sequence unfolds, the mysteries of the organism are both unveiled and sustained. If the reproductive system brings me and my wand to an upright indistractible focus, obliterating time, the set of remaining contiguous images establishes context, to stabilize my hot racing heart and give me back a future. What does prosody do? Prosody turns the pages to reveal the combined systems in their parts, in order to see the poem in its entirety as a transparent matrix of active elements making meaning in concert. It is the botany of a flower-strewn bank, the anatomy of a galloping horse, the etymology of a drunken lexical stew, all together performing their scrutiny as the act of attention we might call "reading a poem."

***

Those are the four beginnings — rather Talmudic, I know, but doesn't Prosody share with the Rabbis a clear-eyed rapture for nuance, and a trust in the text as endlessly resonant, source and resource? But let me back up, to the title before the beginnings, to address not just "Why Prosody?" but specifically why "Prosody Now?" Over the dozen or so years in which I taught the course (its subtitle was *The Meaning of Form*) when I told people what I was teaching the most frequent and consistent response was, "Great. Young people don't know anything about meter and scansion; they need to learn" — as if the only proper site for such inquiry were the traditional mode of counted and stressed syllables. But don't Prosody's features change as forms change?

So "Prosody Now" (I started to write "Paradise Now") suggests a range of post-metrical formal features constructing meaning in the poem, in rough parallel to the old measures wrought by sonnets or hexameters.

A living art transforms its features as history turns and skins shed, and more so under the lasting modernist impulse of, say, Pound's "Make it New" or Diaghilev-to-Cocteau's "Etonnez moi!" or Stein's rose-is-a-rose syntax bomb: "When the language was new — as it was with Chaucer and Homer," she lectures, "the poet . . . could say 'O moon', 'O sea', 'O love', and the moon and the sea and love were really there." But by her time, they'd become "worn out literary words" lacking "intensity," and having lost "the excitingness of pure being." She adds:

> Now listen! I'm no fool. I know that in daily life we don't go around saying '. . . is a . . . is a . . . is a . . .' Yes, I'm no fool; but I think that in that line the rose is red for the first time in English poetry for a hundred years."[4]

And so the shape-shifted forms with their new terminological hats (note to self: *excitingnessence*) ask for Prosody's admiring eye to bring them into fullness. The new poems — whose raised intensities, let's say, aim to bring woodbine and musk roses into perfumed presence for the first time in four hundred years — may not rely on meter and rhyme; their stanzas may be irregular or hidden or turned into paragraphs, and their operations occult. Prosodic features now might include performed silences, interruptions, and fragmentations; syntactic patterning; structural repetitions; a host of dynamic inter-textualities from collage and erasure to homophonic transliterations and lexical inversions; and a long set of original constraints employed mathematically, grammatically, improvisationally, indeterminately, and involuntarily.

For a closer look, here's a poem from my book *Involuntary Lyrics*,[5] whose constraint employs the line-ending words of Shakespeare's sonnets. Lyric on the left, sonnet on the right:

LXXIII. SONNET 73

a red lamp in the green of the night rest
head on his chest be hold
tight by him on fire

or hang

from neck as lie
like vertical weight off cold
toes warming day's breath expire
where he sang
through lungs by
breathing day
go or night come strong
in silence this west-
ern shore house bed with him on
   long
that trail away

That time of the year thou mayst in me behold
When yellow leaves, or none, or few, do hang
Upon those boughs which shake against the
   cold,
Bare ruin'd choirs, where late the sweet birds
   sang.
In me thou see'st the twilight of such day
As after sunset fadeth in the west,
Which by and by black night doth take away,
Death's second self, that seals up all in rest.
In me thou see'st the glowing of such fire
That on the ashes of his youth doth lie,
As the death-bed whereon it must expire
Consumed with that which it was nourish'd by
This thou perceivest, which makes thy love
   more strong,
To love that well which thou must leave ere
   long.

For each Lyric, the lines end with the same words — in fact the rhyme words — as a corresponding sonnet, though I changed the order so that the rhymes *wouldn't* close, separated by enough lineated space that one couldn't really hear their pairing, or at least only occasionally, or at least *testing* the limits of what one does and doesn't hear.

The grid on the following page illustrates the structural correspondence, sonnet to lyric:

What, prosodically, does such a structure do? Some of the resulting (or determining) features include variable line lengths as a means of separating the rhyme words and syncopating the measure; extremely compressed and jumpy syntax governed by the end-words already in place at the start and powered by their largely monosyllabic weights; hyphenations and loosened forms of tense and agreement to allow a minimum of change to the given words; a shadow governance provided by the Shakespeare lexicon and, to a degree, Shakespearean diction high and low;

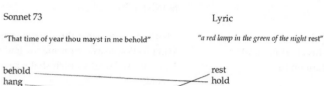

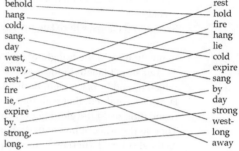

Fig. 1. Grid, sonnet to lyric

a general lack of punctuation to enable syntactic fluidity as required by the words already set; and of course some shadow pressure from sonnet structure itself related to compression *of thought* and line limit. The effect? A feeling of synaptic speed or conversational flow, a joyride of colloquial and elevated usage fostering a sense of person in action and in mind. What I want to suggest here is the range and multiplicity of applied intensities — attended intensities — for one occasion, one poem — that we can also see as compositional: writer — rather than reader — centric.

In fact the origin of the constraint for the Lyrics lay in a prosodic quandary or challenge, as I declared my surfeit with Projective Verse's obsession with line breaks — wasn't there another way through versification — and conceived the new rules by which the line-endings were already set, either as a rest point or a leaping point, words toward which I could gather steam but which I couldn't *choose*. Thus, in effect, the break was already there. As I put it in the afterword to *Involuntary Lyrics,*

44

With these moored but mutated determinants the lines turn on a hinge (sometimes there's just the hinge), projective only in the sense of being shot toward Shakespeare's word already waiting there. A new measure is unloosed — vertiginous but restrained . . .

In addition, my rules of composition included the Quotidian: a suggestion that the poem would be porous to daily life, including the moment at hand. "I wanted 'involuntary,'" I wrote,

> to include what experience was doing to me. The quotidian acts as a given, just as Shakespeare's language is given to the poem. . . . Alternating modes high or low, meditative or notational, [Lyrics] attempt to balance what's being given: the measure of attention. The *tension* of attention.

"Ballasted by the end-words," I explained, "the *Lyrics* fuse incursions from the left hand to the fixed but floating stations of the right." I was holding in mind the image of playing the piano, where one hand acts as the base note, the beat, the chord, i.e. the end word, and the other hand runs up and down the keys in arpeggios and melodic riffs. I wrote *into* the preset end-words, and then negotiated the ensuing stop or the jump across to the next line. A few years earlier, deep in the throes of an immersion in Chopin, whose études, preludes and ballades were teaching me how to write, I met and had a mad fling with a soft-haired cold-hearted man who played piano well — that is what he did well — but for whom I nevertheless harbored this delirious fantasy: I would sit in his lap at the piano while he played Chopin *around* me — me the tone deaf, now a conduit for the master's lavish harmonies and tender melodies. With *Involuntary Lyrics* I sat in my own lap: I was also the piano player. As the virtuoso sweeps aside his tuxedo tails and wiggles his butt like a duck to center it on the piano bench, so I settled myself for composition, listing the rhyme words down the page in a straight vertical line for good posture. Then I hunkered into the seat of my chair, arms relaxed and limber, ready to fly across the keyboard in a crescendo, or jump the end of the line. *Kinetics* became part of the act — and whaddya know didn't Olson's Projectivism come back in anyway, "the *kinetics* of the thing."

Here is a page from my notebook, so you can see the prosodic back-
bone of derived words and how the poem flowed from and toward
them, followed by the poem typeset as it appeared in the book.

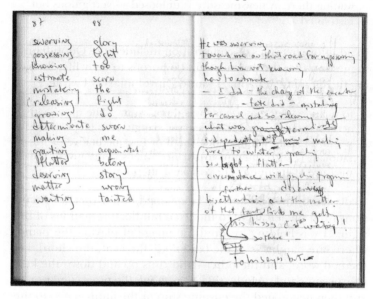

Fig. 2. Notebook page, *Involuntary Lyrics*

LXXXVII.

He was swerving
toward me on that road for my possessing
though him not knowing
how to estimate
I did — the charge of the encounter — *fate* did — mistaking
for casual and so releasing
what was already growing
independently, indeterminate
to his eyes but — *I* knew, making
sure to water, granting
sunlight, flatter
circumstance with psychic tropism deserving
his further attention intrigued and the matter
of the fact now finds me getting his kisses I was wanting!

Lastly, vocabulary itself was a determining factor: since I didn't choose the end words they were actually a feature of form — there not for what they said, but for the spatial position they occupied — a feature that nevertheless fed what the *Lyrics* were about: "Didn't erotics bleed right through," the footnote suggests, "with so much incidence of direct address and all those cruisy 'eyes'?" The sonnets, from their private occasion, tossed up bouquets of "thee" and "thine" with some abandon, and the love-drunk or lovesick sonnet "eyes" were ever-present, appearing as they do in some thirty percent of the sonnets. Because I had to use those words, my Lyrics, inevitably, were similarly besotted, framed by a face-to-face starry-eyed gaze.

To bring it home, then: A full prosodic account of *Involuntary Lyrics* as an act of composition, writing *or* reading, would register the impact — the *increase* — of all these converging elements on what we call meaning, now wholly transmogrified by the mash.

And that is *one* version of *one* constraint to suggest *some* of the parallels between the old forms and new variations. Many more are operative: Where there were fixed meters now there are fixed numerical as well as textual constraints; where there were dropped feet now there are pure elisions, empowered silences; where there was rhyme now there are patterned repetitions of flowering syntax and parts of speech; where there was scansion now there is "tone leading of vowels" or composing "in the sequence of the musical phrase" or the lovely head-banging "deterministic non-intentionality."

Thus, "Prosody Now," its viability and its utility. For the course in Prosody — pedagogy likes clarity — I devised a methodology to separate and isolate some of the strands: Each week or two we focused on one basic element, illustrated with examples classic and contemporary, narrowing the frame to better hone our attention. These divisions were the six "powers" of Image, Line, Structure, Grammar, Repetition, and Silence, also known as Space. (This last rubric, by the way, was forever anecdotally attached to a young San Francisco queen of our hippy days — a slip of a thing with long black streaming hair who, when you chanced to meet on the street and ask how he was doing, would literally twirl in a circle as he whipped his hair around and answer, "s=p=a=c=i=o=u=s!" I always wanted to go from Structure to Grammar to Repetition to *Spacious* . . .)

But beyond that the course was conceived along my encyclopedic model — it was *Britannicated*— (don't stop me now!) — as a set of six transparencies in sequence, to construct a semester-long reading of a set of "core poems" as an adventure in parsing and composing. In addition to the Princeton and the handout-illustrations, I'd chosen these dozen or so pieces — poems I admired — as the "core" text to measure prosody's route of augmentation: We read the poems at the first class for pure "content," and then returned under the narrowed lens of each governing figure (Image, Line, etc.) to chart its specific contributing force. Each week or so a new element to consider; each week the core poems considered *only* in the light of that given element.

At the end, a poem having been examined at every stop to see the ways in which meaning was activated by one component, we returned to the reassembled poem in all its semantic density to see it anew as a complex stack of concurrent inciters. The red-in-a-century rose revealed as a swarm of love-me love-me-not petals. The poem's meaning, straightforward at the start of the semester, became, by the end, a many-minded, many-legged, multi-phasic, polyamorous power enlivened by a host of structural pressures to raise the mystery of its smile and put a glimmer in its eyes.

What is Prosody? It is the face and form by which the poem falls more deeply in love with meaning . . . and the body through which writer and reader are drawn into the embrace.

[2012]

Notes

1. William Shakespeare, *A Midsummer Night's Dream*, Act II, scene 2.

2. Alex Preminger and T. V. F. Brogan, eds., *The New Princeton Encyclopedia of Poetry and Poetics*, Princeton University Press, 1993, p. 982 ff.

3. Alex Preminger and T. V. F. Brogan, eds., *The New Princeton Encyclopedia of Poetry and Poetics*, p. 987.

4. Gertrude Stein, *Look at Me Now and Here I Am*, Penguin Books, 1967, p. 7.

5. Aaron Shurin, *Involuntary Lyrics*, Omnidawn, 2005.

Note to a Student

Dear Annie —

From time to time I like to pull back and take a macrocosmic view, instead of critiquing the pieces of a poem, and that's what I'm doing today with your "theory." It's not that it works better or less better than other poems, it's just that I think maybe I can be more useful approaching things from another angle — So I haven't marked up the poem, really, to question *asymptote* or *osculating*, or to admire the meeting of foot, floor, and distance . . .

Basically, it's become clear to me that you're just too smart for your poetry now — so the challenge is how to get you to be a little stupider. If that doesn't sound so attractive, another way of putting it is that because you have such joy in philosophical mindedness I think maybe you think your poem should be thus delighted. But in fact you may be like a philosophy stage mother, pushing your poem to solve the problems you always wanted to solve. What if your poem really wants to fix cars or go surfing — what if it is a *really great* surfer, with a gift for vertiginous stanzas and precipitous line breaks and a feel for the wind? Or let's compare you to a fine esthete of a gay man — two ballet queens in fact — who adopt a daughter who, it turns out, only wants to play with trucks and fix cars (again with the cars!) — in between boxing bouts that is — but with a ballet master's knowledge of footwork and balance, and a boundless, pugilist anger rooted in world pain. But you want to make her put on a tutu and take dance classes.

Flaubert, you know, when he set himself the task of composing a new kind of novel — *Madame Bovary* — basically tied his hands behind his back so that all the gestures he was fond of — his *natural* gestures — were forbidden to him — all his favorite orientalisms and baroque embellishments, forcing him to discover a clearer-eyed prose that fit the disenchanted conditions of the nineteenth century, and changed fiction forever.

I think your natural gesture may be the poem's intellection, following your own superior intellectualism. If I say *stop thinking* I mean *let the poem think*. If I say *poem think* I mean *line, image, measure, rhythm, vowel tone,* and *syntax*. If you have ideas and theory — and, bless you, you do — work with them, on them, discuss them, have study groups around them, and then write poems that pretend to look the other way (because they never can, but need to be caught unaware by ideas). I mean once you get *in,* your intellect will be there to manifest however — you will be you — but you have to get in with a feint, you have to *follow*. Or think of forms, always form, to find a translation of means, as if a baseball player who was secretly a cosmologist found the arcs and rotations of the stars in the trajectories of a spinning leather ball, calculated only to the vectors of glove and bat: the properties of the form of his art. He thinks about *them,* not the stars.

I take it as a given that you have such feel for the poem's energy and parts. You have a wonderful, careful ear, you have open emotional resources (if not always directly attached to the solar plexus), you have an eye for the line's place in the page's space . . . and at least a general belief that all of these are real agents of meaning. Do you believe they are the *only* agents of poetic meaning? No, not yet . . . but, in fact, they are! The poem can't be your mule — in either sense: it can't carry the load of your ideas on its back up the hill, and you can't stuff it inside so it can carry your philosophy like contraband across into the realm of poetic meaning. It won't carry and it can't be stuffed. I think you know this, but you're constantly tempted. But if you can stay still, and calm your mind into a light stupidity, you can catch the poem passing like some streaming soul on its way to incarnation, and, given that you'll be empty rather than full, you can fuse with it and, for some duration, find, which is to say make, meaning together. Which will be new to both: A collaboration.

[2011]

II.

II

Active Form

Toward a Gay/Lesbian Poetics

There's a potential for social activism within the parameters of
writing itself that interests me, interior to the text, interior to
the sentence; one that attacks the authoritarianism of syntax
and tense, of pronouns and subject identity — those sites of
gender control, linear thinking, dominance hierarchies, and
social ideology.

Though less inflected (infected) than other languages, English still elementalizes gender with inflexible pronouns (he/
she), foregrounding characteristics we're appalled by, for example, in the case of race. We won't tolerate the inclusion of
race-specific terms when they have nothing to do with the intended story, but look the other way when gender is named. But
if writing unthinkingly splits its persons into groups whose social
formation is based on political and economic inequality, and a
whole range of inaccurate sexual typing, does that writing challenge or serve the social order? Third-person singular pronouns
— the male/female indicators — impose on people, under the
guise of biological imperative, the complete baggage of gender
ideology.

Traditional use of "voice" and point of view in narration
— who is speaking or writing — proposes a fixed identity: the
unified subject, an inhibiting convenience that serves to keep
readers and writers in place, in assigned roles, "me" or "you."
How useful is this egocentric model; how do pronouns control
our own perception of experience so that we learn not to shift
among related mutable frameworks and get locked into indi-
vidualism, forced to view the changing universe — the true Col-
lective — as something distinct and apart from ourselves?

Other loaded concerns: active over passive constructions, topic sentences and a hierarchical construction of meaning, the refraction and subjugation of time through tense. With such rules for writing, receptivity is trashed out, answers are favored over questions — always a suspect maneuver — and history is forced into the background as an element of the past, not the present. Confronting these issues as they appear in the hidden inheritance of correct form forces the reader to actively enter the text. And to awaken attention in the reader is to construct responsibility — the ability to respond, a primary requirement for social change.

How might these issues relate to gay/lesbian experience, and how might they begin to inform a gay/lesbian poetics, the way women's experiences might have described a poetics of gender? We might take a clue from feminist critiques that seek to define an "other" writing — initially a writing of "otherness" — that poses itself against patriarchal models, to discover a route out of the linear, or the binary, and into . . . what? Catharine Stimpson points to the example of Gertrude Stein, who

> was searching for the elementary particles of language, no matter how many of them there might be. The process is so wonderfully messy, the product so multi-textured, that together they challenge two patterns of thought on which gender depends: binarism, splitting the world into mutually reinforcing sets of dualistic categories, including that of feminine/masculine; and teleologicalism, believing that the world, and its narratives, spin toward certain ends, including the triumph of the willful masculine over the feminine.[1]

Lyn Hejinian also points to Stein's decentralized texts, suggesting an inheritance from Cézanne, whose

> landscapes are presented, so to speak, broadside, and more than one area is present with full force. Similarly, Stein distributes value or meaning across the widest possible range of articulation—in this context, one might say, panoramically.[2]

And Elaine Showalter uses the collage metaphor of the quilt for women's writing, "piecing" small fragments into a pattern, and "patching" them into a design, and stitching them together, with analogies to language use first on the level of the sentence, then in terms of the structure of a story or novel, and finally the images, motifs, or symbols . . . that unify a fictional work.[3]

Homosexuality and gender are not the same, but they are related. Like feminism, gay and lesbian experiences are predicated on an otherness, an alienation from the dominant model of social integration. Unlike feminism, they are also ("homo") based on sameness, not a subjugation but an equality of affection. Both gay men and lesbians inhabit and reinhabit gender, transforming it to their own likenesses. I believe in this aspect we share a common situation: both in and out of gender, migrated from our birthplaces, empowered by the transgression. We do not fit; by not fitting we are freed.

What are the virtues of these special circumstances, what inner sanctums do they give entrée to? The trans-gender experience — the heightened awareness of gender-role-playing, the feeling of being outside of part of gender (its sanctioned oppositional dualities), of actual cross dressing beloved of queens and dykes both — will these lead us to, afford us the opportunities of, releasing ourselves from the idea of the unified subject, from the constrictions of pronouns, and into shape shifting in syntax? Outside of traditional tradition as we are — the nuke family and its capital consumerism — can we keep that quicksilver in the sentence, avoid the hierarchy of tenses, step as lightly in language as we can in the streets? We might find a writing that is itself a model for community, like Rachel Blau DuPlessis's vision,

> breaking hierarchical structures, making an even display of elements over the surface with no climactic place or movement, having the materials organized into many centers.[4]

The experience of homosexuality is not circumscribed by powerlessness; it includes a dynamic act of power — coming out — that blasts the walls of the fixed subject — "I can't change" — with a discriminating confidence that says "I'm not that" — and recreates identity in the service of an erotic and affectionate ideal. Luce Irigaray uses a female biological model to explain a dynamic relationship to language:

> Woman has sex organs just about everywhere. She experiences pleasure just about everywhere. The geography of her pleasure is much more diversified, more multiple in its differences, more complex, more subtle, than is imagined . . . "She" is infinitely other in herself. That is undoubtedly the reason she is called temperamental, incomprehensible, perturbed, capricious — not to mention her language in which "she" goes off in all direction . . . In her statements . . . woman retouches herself constantly.[5]

But the sexuality of gay men is also more diversified than imagined, and perhaps closer to female experience than some realize; unlike most heterosexual men it also includes multiple sites of arousal — nipples, assholes, mouths, fingers, and fists as well as cocks, and prioritizes both oral and anal receptivity. "A cock's pleasure," says Robert Glück in a pre-AIDS challenge,

> is like a fist, concentrated; anal pleasure is diffused, an open palm, and the pleasure of an anal orgasm is founded on relaxation. It's hard to understand how a man can write well if he doesn't like to be fucked. There's no evidence to support this theory; still, you can't be so straight that you don't submit to pleasure.[6]

In my dream, a gay/lesbian poetics would be polymorphous perverse, shot through with arousal, crescendo and release, rhythm, and repetition, and constructive of meaning when touched anywhere. Lyn Heijinian asks,

> Can form make the primary chaos . . . articulate without depriving it of its capacious vitality, and its generative power? Can form go even further than that and actually generate that potency, opening uncertainty to curiosity, incompleteness to speculation, and turning vastness into plenitude? . . . This is, in fact the function of form in art. Form is not a fixture but an activity.[7]

An *activism,* I would add. As gay and lesbian writers, we need to have the courage of our acts.

[1990]

Notes

1. Catharine Stimpson, in *The Poetics of Gender,* Nancy K. Miller, ed. Columbia University Press, 1986, p. 4.

2. Lyn Hejinian, "Grammar and Landscape," *Temblor* 33, 1986, p. 136.

3. Elaine Showalter, in Stimpson, *The Poetics of Gender,* p. 223.

4. Rachel Blau DuPlessis, in *The Poetics of Gender,* p. 226.

5. Luce Irigaray, in *Feminist Criticism and Social Change,* Judith Newton and Deborah Rosenfelt, eds., Methuen, 1985, p. 89.

6. Robert Glück, *Elements of a Coffee Service,* Four Seasons Foundation, 1982, p. 33.

7. Lyn Heijinian, "The Rejection of Closure," *Poetics Journal* 34, Women and Language, 1984, p. 137.

Writing into the Twenty-First Century

The question of the millennium has been made largely moot in my life by the AIDS pandemic, which has found many of my friends meeting their millennia early. They have — we have — been much too surrounded by the Present, and the Present has been much too full of our Past. Personal mortality has a way of inscribing its own significators, and century markers seem arbitrary in comparison. Under instructions from my community-mates, I've been learning to attend what's at hand — my own hand, for instance, before my face; so close to my face it's the little lines one usually doesn't see that I'm reading, finer and finer as they dissolve the flesh into its ever rarer structures . . .

And, anyway, whose millennium? Likely as not I'd find another point of origin if I were to celebrate. Why not start counting from the Venus of Willendorf, say, or at least, writerly, from *Gilgamesh* or Homer? As for centuries . . . OK: I'm a nineteenth-century Romantic poet with postmodern hands. If I do follow this millennialism, does that mean I'll have to come up with a new epoch-oriented term to describe my writing? Oy.

I couldn't predict how anyone else would play this writing out. I can't predict how I will play it out — given, especially, intentionality's sad overload, that poor poor prognosticator. I've never really had a poetics except insofar as my writing has made me have one. In other words, by the time my ideologies have entered the poem the poem has made *them*. I attend writing (H.D.'s ever-present "Take me anywhere, anywhere; I walk into you. . . ."[1]). I can explain to you later how my compositional mind has synthesized experience, and build on that.

To return to the problem of that hand and its coiled energies, or to those coiled energies which appear in the form of a hand. It is/they are a marker for a tense set of oppositions I'm continually writing into, to pose third — or more — embracing alternatives, and smash that double-faced monster (the monster is duality itself) before it can turn its same other face. I'm about ten years through a pursuit of the prose poem and its enmeshing of story and anti-story, its obvious enwebbing of lineation and sentences. [Here I want to make a Mosaic statement like Pound or Olson: the line is dead. Question: What is the new line?] I'm charmed by narrative and narrative tropes, but especially by how they can be troubled by the sensuous eruptions lyric proposes — or vice versa — and I wonder if, how and why historical periods favor one mode over the other. [Question: Why has gay fiction eaten gay poetry?]

Similarly, my work is florid and verbose while it's also disjunct and filled with ellipses. [Question: How are misogyny and homophobia encoded in American minimalism?] Subjectivity, that restless noodle, keeps spreading toward the Other's point of view, and gender, *that* biocultural collision, wants to be written in gradational shifts impossible to fix. [Question: How do we compose socially informed writing that at the same time confronts and transgresses social, psychological, and moral taboos?]

These and many other questions, more questions, beautiful shapely questions. They come at once from every direction. "It is dawn at Jerusalem," says Pound, "while midnight hovers above the Pillars of Hercules. All ages are contemporaneous. . . . This is especially true of literature, where the real time is independent of the apparent, and where many dead men are our grandchildren's contemporaries. . . ."[2]

An open palm signals, then pulls you in. O Millennium, you gorgeous cataclysmic new thing, aren't you always here at hand? Take me anywhere. I walk into you. "Walk," as H.D. says, "unfalteringly toward a Lover, / *the hachish supérieur* of dream."

[1993]

Notes

1. H.D., *Hermetic Definition*, New Directions, 1972, p. 4 ff.
2. Ezra Pound, *The Spirit of Romance*, New Directions, p. 8.

61

Queerly

AIDS and the Queer Imagination

I thought the easiest way for me to talk about AIDS and the queer imagination is to reference briefly my new book, *Unbound*, subtitled *A Book of AIDS*.

Unbound tries to suggests a variety of surprising even oblique ways in which AIDS relates to our lives on a daily, even hourly, basis. I hoped to show how writing about AIDS — imagining AIDS I might say for this panel — could find its route along the most tangential — I might say queerest — paths, and still arrive at what I've called "the viral core."

For example, in a piece from the book called "My Memorial," I'm listening to opera arias and classical music, spontaneously and melodramatically imagining the music that might be played at my own memorial, as I've heard such music played at the memorials of so many friends. The circumstances of listening to music like this are in no way AIDS specific; the piece in fact becomes a meditation on music itself, and the power of music, and how when we love a piece of music — we all know this from love affairs and "our song" — we somehow, forever after, reside there, in the music. We become what we listen to. I was listening to Montserrat Caballé sing an aria or my favorite violinist Dmitry Sitkovetsky play Bach's solos, but the quality of my listening, the way in which I was engaged to enter more deeply into the music and think about my or anyone's relation to music in a new way, was, in fact, entirely transformed by AIDS, though it had nothing to do with the music I was listening to. I'd been pushed deeper in from an odd angle out. AIDS has queered my imagination.

In another piece in *Unbound* I'm cruising through Buena Vista Park after last year's great storm, and looking at the downed trees — "fallen giants," I say — and think of my friends — those giants — who've fallen to the storm of AIDS. I was just walking in the park. There's a guy there I know casually and in casual conversation he mentions how it's nice to see me again after a while, indicating — most of us know this routine — that when one doesn't see someone for a while one suspects illness or more. But we were just cruising in the park. I see some grass growing on one of those fallen tree trunks and am reminded of friends' miraculous struggles, of new drugs and resurrections and the enormity as well as the impermanence of death. So my little walk in the park to cruise or sun myself became a meditation on mortality, because AIDS has queered my imagination.

Another piece talks about sitting at a café drinking coffee and seeing the ghosts of friends walk through, so I do a double take when — you get the rhythm now I think — I was just drinking coffee. Then I'm in a meditation on haunting, and really what fulfilling a life means. AIDS has even queered my damn coffee!

What I'm trying to suggest is the totality, the intricacy, the always surprising grievousness *and* the improbable beauty of AIDS, how thoroughly it's affected not just our lives in experiential ways but our poetic and creative imaginations, raising meaning out of strange minimal details, and turning daily insignificant moments into philosophical discourses.

What's important for me to suggest further about this complexity is that we're neither early nor late in the epidemic because the imagination is not located in time (though it dances with time.) Don't let anybody say — as they've said to me — *another* book about AIDS? If anyone asks — as they've asked me — why write about AIDS now — as if it were comfortably in the past — think not just of HIV status and you or your friends' current struggles but of the all ways AIDS has impacted and still impacts your life, your ideas, your dreams. This information is so rare, so local, so unchosen, so thorough, so detailed, so profound — that it's crucial information many people don't have access to. I mean the experience of AIDS, communally and individually, is a monumental experience of meaning. Its effect on the queer imagination has been to queer us all even further, to sail us outward along the edges we already refine, taking nothing for granted, attending the moment, and imagining what we may have already guessed, that this perspective from the radical margins is really central, core territory.

[1996]

Lo How I Vanysshe

Afterword to Codex

from "Codex"

Now the sluices are a penchant for status and the bright eye
of the coin. WHEEL HIM FOLDED INTO A RESTAURANT HE'LL
TEASE THE WAITRESS ABOUT HER BREASTS, an insight of the
grasp of his hand. Not to nod to in the vigor of assent defends
the contract in a pit, "*and the inner wall it has no equal,*" neither the combine nor HIS SUBDIVISIONS BY THE SEA. A luxury
holdover the egg canapé slid on the floor warts a position in
the wager, lays an unction inside a scoop "*the night lapped over
them.*" Soldered in uniform cranked on a bayonet, woods his
little steps forward "not a dreamer, a schemer" "*he held up his
arms for a mast*" as the winds blew over him

This is the saddest poem I ever wrote. This is the scariest poem
I ever wrote. The saddest line is: "'*he held up his arms for a mast*'
as the winds blew over him." My father is unaided naked, and
completely externalized.

In the typographical weave of "Codex" capital letters enact his
desperate grasp through the surface, pulling as if through power of will his attenuating narrative line.

A woven thread ascends and descends.

I had been reading *The Epic of Gilgamesh,* and started to bracket
particular gnomic phrases which seemed to speak, almost ge-
nerically, from a mythic voice. Ultimately, these were typed,
snipped, put in an envelope, and drawn out at indeterminate

points to (re)determine the poem by interruption and sway. (Written in 1983/84, "Codex" stands as the beginning of a collage methodology I have pursued in various orders for twelve years since.)

But there was more shade than that. The descent of Gilgamesh into the Sumerian underworld ghosted my composition, so that, as my father appeared instantly in the poem, I knew where I would be guiding him. The scariest line is: "HE'S BARGAINING WITH THE FERRYMAN FOR A QUARTER ON THE MILE." The man brought to judgment who doesn't know he's being brought to judgment is colder than naked.

If he's not my father, name him yourself, you are invited.

Did I think I could guide him through hell without going there too? Had I lived all the hell I needed to having lived with him and thus inured? In the end I was protected only by faith in poetry's purity of judgment, where Innana could read in my composing eyes the difference between father and son. The poem was my protective skin. My mother had already died of a massive heart attack and could no longer stand between.

Language spews as if from just such a ruptured organ. My father blew out language so he might hear it, emptily, in the air, and read in the imagined shape of his utterances a journey out of the grandfather's *shtetl.* An almost goofy pompousness — it might have been comic — was wedded to a mimic's ear. It was the wrong way — sorely underestimated — to use language, but it helped make of two sons two poets with no underestimation of the powers of language, and other textured ways to trumpet "sound."

By 1984 new shadows were already in the air — seepage up from — and several people I knew had died of AIDS. Looking backward, it's impossible to extricate the one prelude from the other denouement. The underworld and the overworld were interpenetrating.

In 1986 my father died, also of a heart attack. Having written him through "Codex," I had nothing left to demand of him, and stood by in the hospital room where I sponged his body and counted his failing breaths. He held on so the remaining family could all gather around, giving us — his grace — the chance — our grace — to *be* there.

When the poem says "remember me to my mother," I originally wanted that last word to be written in Chaucerian English, as in:

> And on the ground, which is my moodres gate,
> I knokke with my staf, bothe erly and late,
> And seye 'Leeve mooder leet me in!
> Lo how I vanysshe, flessh, and blood, and skyn! . . .

I wrote the poem well before his dying. But the urgency was unavoidable, and truculent enough to cut cuneiform wedges in clay tablets. "The descent beckons," as Williams says. Gilgamesh turned to the underworld to recover love.

[1995]

Note

Aaron Shurin, *Codex*, Meow Press, 1997.

Binding *Unbound*

An Introduction to Unbound:
A Book of AIDS

Among the literary texts and talks collected here that arose alongside my poetry in a heady period of theory and critique — flowering in particular after my studies in poetics at New College of California — *Unbound* is at the heart of the matter. The penetrating sorrow of AIDS, the shock, the depth charge, the limitlessness ("unbound"), the arc of inquiry, the angels, the call to order, the call to death, the call to life: all these passions of the epidemic pulled at my essay writing as of some primal eros or anti-eros. They demanded the figure of a mortal body to house their contending forces. As the human body was the form in which the meaning of the virus found agency, so my writing about the epidemic would shape itself toward bodies as a formal principle. In other words, the analysis — the *poetic* analysis — would be channeled through people in time and space — in *history* — and the essays in *Unbound* would structure themselves as a new (to me) kind of poetic *narrative*, where revelations were attached to actual names, and the viral ink documented its transit in the stories and speeches of my friends who were its actual hosts.

My poetry had already engaged the form of the prose-poem to unwind mini-narratives, queered by radical ellipsis and mysteriously free-floating subjectivity, but *Unbound*, with its urgent figures and voices, led me toward a critical writing that was also housed in narrative. I had, in fact, already committed myself to the first-person voice even in critical writing, as a means of destabilizing authority and undermining the fiction of objectivity.

No high-floating blind statements of supposed facts, or pseudo-neutral, "One could say that . . ." Bent along the informing angles of gender, queerness, and identity formation, the speaking subject with a house of skin and bones would be my petitioner. Mine was not going be a disembodied poetics! But with its information inextricably linked to the lives of my friends, AIDS raised the stakes to make neutrality impossible and subjectivity *comprehensive.*

And yet, as much as "body" absorbed "theory" into its membranes, theory demanded that body be symbolic, multi-focal, historicized, and self-analytical (or should I say self-diagnostic?) Skin would be informed by meaning, and meaning by skin. From the beginning the essays in *Unbound* were viewed as part of my work in poetics, exactly as the guiding impulse at the root of my inquest was a search through the bones of the epidemic for poetic meaning. I wanted information subtler than statistics, deeper than diagnosis, more pitched than mourning, rawer than memory and richer than fact, grander than benedictions . . . ignited by a mortal fire but outlasting it. I wanted to wrest a poem's meaning from the epidemic's prose — the quotidian facts, the journalism, the indexed obituaries. And I wanted to use prose to dissect the epidemic, and lay bare its poetic heart: the quoted language of transcendence, the angelic clarity and sorrowful wisdom. Almost to the end, in fact, the subtitle of *Unbound* was, "A Poetics of AIDS." (Its actual working title was a resonant but unfortunate phrase taken from one of the essays: *Mortal Purposes.* Alas I kept saying to myself, "*Myrtle Porpoises,*" and had to send both purpose and porpoise back to the blue wild . . .) *Unbound* took shape in the grip of personal narrative, balancing daily fact and daily awe, and the flare of poetic attention, fusing the familiar and the extraordinary.

The circumstances were overripe with emotion, and easily overwhelming, and I didn't have scientific distance — medical or social. Poetics also meant the angle *in.* I had in mind a passage from Claude Lanzmann's holocaust documentary *Shoah,* in which Polish townsfolk accept culpability for a particularly brutal and efficient extermination process because Lanzmann asks them questions of such specificity that they get lost in the details and forget the larger guilt — details, for example, about the carpentry and measurements of what is essentially an execution platform. AIDS cut such a wide and jagged swath across our lives (I want to say its scythe did) that I sought to enter at an angle or an edge, often arriving on the associative vibrations of literature and art: the reverberations of a pictorial image or a quoted line. *Unbound* is replete with citations from my contributing heroes Shakespeare, Chaucer, Whitman, Proust, Stein, and Cocteau; with evocations of the music of Chopin and Verdi, of the golden throat of Montserrat Caballé or the violet eyes of Elizabeth Taylor; with examinations of photographs in single and in sequence, and articulations of the dancer *and* the dance. The pieces partook of my life in letters and art because they partook of my life in letters and art. The impulse was holistic. The subtitle ultimately became "A Book of AIDS" much as if it had been a day book or a book of hours, where AIDS was equal to the day or the hour.

Almost all of the writing in *Unbound* appeared in the same journals and presses that were publishing my poetry. I was aggressively determined that this writing be seen as central to my literary work; I was uniformly insistent that I lacked the luxury to frame another discourse; and I was achingly aware that those not inside the circle of fire had very little idea of the intensity and the enormity of the flames. And so *Unbound* was published in book form by the fine literary press Sun & Moon, which had already published my poetry collection *Into Distances*. The essays appeared in *Poetics Journal, Talisman, Temblor* and *ACTS*. I should say with respect that though I came armed for battle, the editors of these publications met me with high interest and regard. Nevertheless there was very little other writing related to AIDS appearing in these journals, and if I sometimes felt ferociously isolated, the isolated circumstances fueled my ferocity. I had already published and read a fair amount of homo-centric work in the same or similar venues, behind an imaginary "I know what I'm talking about so shut up and listen" guard, and I used to joke admiringly that the largely hetero audiences actually did. In truth many of the barriers I blew down were internal, but in any event they were downed.

Unbound formed in the clearing as a series of inquiries and interjections, a rising arc inside a descending spiral, a way out that was a way in. And if I have given the impression that my endeavors were somehow heroic, it is a fiction of the shorthand of my telling. I agonized over how to write; I was late to the task; I trembled nervously over the transcendental gifts my friends had given me. But I was surrounded by what I might properly call a sense of duty, even if it at times it felt like nowhere to run: AIDS chased me down, cornered me, and stuck a pen in my hand.

[2014]

Note

Aaron Shurin, *Unbound: A Book of AIDS*, Sun & Moon Press, 1997.

71

From *Unbound*

A Book of AIDS

Preface

Around 1982 a young man I knew opened up his mouth and showed me the deep inside of his upper palate where a few pale areas represented Kaposi's sarcoma. His mouth was dark — ah, sweet vulnerability! — and I could barely detect (we were at work, no flashlight) the differences in shading he spoke of. That fearful subtlety was so telling his mouth — dark oracle — remains open before me: I'm still listening to what it has to say.

I'm still writing into what it has to say. The *range* of information AIDS presents keeps one at full attention. Who knew, to begin, what dimensions the replicate virus would come to occupy? The various works collected here are the stations of an enlarging question: the question, alarmed, of a cell aroused by invasion, or the yearning curl of a lover's body awake on the vacated sheets.

There was no project; I've been learning to write about AIDS piece by piece *through* piece by piece. I've dated the texts here, and let facts and figures remain as they were originally, to mark the developing way. But the numbers, their aggregate lines (their additions, multiplications, and subtractions), were not my story. For that reason I call this small but incremental book a poetics: Its way was made with both hands stretched, investigative, crossing and recrossing. The process — poetic, even lyric — tests the threads as it leads them — as it's led by them — and coaxes their meeting, otherwise statistical, toward meaning(s).

Reading backward I seem, now, to have started each piece from ground zero, trying to capture the whole of AIDS in a swipe, from an unanticipated slant. Each time, it seems, some face of mortality was there to surprise me, with its furious broadside view too spacious for my narrow-set eyes, sky-wide and roiling and only just for the moment separate, avoidable. My own ever-baby face receded, as I stood in the shadow and watched the light flame others. The writing progressed as narration.

Authority? — *not* mine, but an urge toward the integration of fear and immutable fact, and a heart for consequence. Who could have moved me to this end but the men whose names are mentioned here, who were my informants and guides, and whose natural affectional alliances made an epidemic based on love and desire possible? It soon became clear that for me writing about AIDS was weighted toward witness. Such participation's cursèd rare privilege is offered to you.

[1996]

Full Circle

Postscript to "City Of Men"

When I read my erotic rampage, "City of Men," to a group of students a couple of years back, one aw-shucks type with wider-than-ever eyes responded: "Boy, that sure isn't safe sex!" Chagrined, I held up the pages, pointing to the poem itself, the act of writing it. "No," I smiled, "*this* is safe sex!" But — chastened — I'd copped out; it was exactly what I had *not* intended with "City of Men."

I did have a hidden agenda. The poem uses only Whitman's language, culled from poems in the "Children of Adam" and "Calamus" groupings from *Leaves of Grass*. As most careful readers of Whitman know, "Calamus" is his collection of homoerotic love poems, emotional, tender, idealistic, radically political, prophetic, obliquely erotic, but — alas — not sexual. If you want sex, go to the grouping "Children of Adam," Whitman's putative heterosexual songs. They are filled with body and body parts, physical material catalogues, paeans to the sex act — but — alas — no love. The body is electric but it is not affectionate.

I have read Whitman's private journals, the most private parts, where they are written partially in code to keep the secret — perhaps from himself as well as others — of his love for Peter Doyle, the secret — but we've heard this many times from the nineteenth and twentieth centuries — torment of his awakening but not yet awake homosexuality, the revelations of his self-expressed desire to (using for homoeroticism his code word "adhesiveness") "depress the adhesive nature / It is in excess — making life a torment / All this diseased, feverish, disproportionate *adhesiveness*." Depress it *in himself!* Anyone who has been there can immediately recognize the call of the closet. This pernicious disregard for truth caught Whitman — in spite of his revolutionary outspokenness about sex and the body as well as male/male affection — and forced him to sever his love poems — his writing of eros — into two mutually exclusive — and incomplete — halves.

My historical period has permitted me to come full circle, to write my eros out of spirit and body, shamelessly, and perhaps for the first time in history from a completely integrated viewpoint. In composing "City of Men" I chose to graft — by interspersing them — poems from Whitman's "Calamus" with those from his "Children of Adam." Where the body in "Calamus" is incessantly hidden, metaphorized as leaves, roots, blossoms, scented herbage, live oak, moss, vines, and buds, now it can be revealed in its polymorphous glory as arms, shoulders, lips, fingers, loins, elbows and necks. No more will we hear — as in "Calamus" — "I dare not tell it in words" or "Here I shade and hide my thoughts"; rather, as in "Children of Adam": "Be not afraid of my body."

It seems essential to me, in the age of AIDS, to keep the body forward, to keep the parts named, to not let ourselves get scared back into our various closets by those who would profit from sexual repression, from sublimation and fear of sex. What losses do we suffer by blindly embracing — if not "compulsive" sex — compulsive dating, compulsive monogamy, compulsive matrimony and domesticity, and when does avoidance of particular sex acts deteriorate into avoidance of creative exploration: dulled nerves, consumerist complacency, couplist or nuclear family paranoia, social scapegoating, stereotyping, and moral sanctimony? Didn't my generation become sexual pioneers not just by increasing the range of permissible sex acts and sex-enacted places but by tying sexual expression to socialism, feminism, national liberation movements, consciousness expansion, legal and individual rights, and radical psychologies, and if it gets squashed what else gets squashed with it? The chaotic force of eros — once called *desire* — is a depth charge for *change*. Contain it and we may live an ordered existence, sure: *following orders*.

So I do *not* propose "City of Men," or any other creative act, as a substitution for sex. I do of course propose safe sex — *medi-*

cally safe but not politically safe, not socially or even psychically safe. And toward the day when the Human Immunodeficiency Virus is consigned to the dustbins of history, I'll dream — with Whitman — "Unscrew the locks from the doors! / Unscrew the doors themselves from their jambs!"

[1988]

Notes from Under

It is alphabetic from the start, as if the full name were too terrible to be spoken, or because we don't want to know the elaboration that would cause a true and necessary engagement with its nature; prefer a modest, even pleasant-sounding acronym to keep it hidden: AIDS. And so it remains a shark fin disease, barely indicated above, red maw gaping beneath the sight line — for those, that is, who live — marginal — beneath the infested sea. If you live here, you know it. If not, have you heard the drowning screaming your names? If not, what constitutes your privilege, and how will you receive my anger?

I am not, here, talking sex, though certainly that sublime loss of self has been threatened with — at least — self-consciousness. I have been immersed in a more quotidian terror, its brunch and coffee dialogues, or dream analogues, or telephone weepings; in community (the Gay, though clearly others are affected — all are affected — the community of affected I know are Gay) conversation, its local pits and searing elevations. So, a cloud of attendant issues and their griefs. Among friends — dead, dying, or scared, the sorrowful healthy — testimony: what I have seen that you must now know, see, for I have been surrounded and among my friends in adversity creating a life, their rising and falling beauties, deaths and tests and imagined fulfilled acts that have unleashed instructions upon us, the uninitiated.

***

For this, reading the world, new language events by which we measure grief and fear; how the virus has made us talk about it — forms of disclosure, witness, vocabularies, stories. A new literary structure I feared becoming master of: the obituary. One's sense of the vanishing, people and — struggle against it as we will (buried alive!) — era. How what we look for first, almost perverse in eagerness, in the Gay weekly papers are the names and photos of those who've died this week. Who and how many did you know, numbers as stripes of honor. "I knew five people this week." And I didn't even know T had been sick till I saw his photo in the obituaries — a thrill with which one engages the paper, surprise building toward their appearance on page 12, to see how much sorrow one can translate into endurance. And cry, continually, because some lover used a nickname for his dead friend — *and* direct address — and it's hard to be impersonal when people are calling each other sweetie across *that* gulf. (I can't — don't want to — say the names of endearment here; I/thou is their only proper usage; what signifies is that the form functions while including the dead.) And, as adjunct language, there are lists: how as a young man — a baby homosexual, I say — I kept a tally of the first men I laid, on one hand (with names), two hands, too many for fingers and toes, finally uncountable. Then, around 1982, the list began of who had died, who was sick, who was sero-positive — soon, too, uncountable. Another fear: the fear of forgetting. With its shadow: the desire to forget.

I'm infected by a vocabulary, a prisoner of its overspecialized agenda. I know OK-T4 helper cells, macrophages, lymphadenopathy, hairy leukoplakia; I know the syntax — the route of congregation — more than the definitions. By how they appear in the sentence I can pretty much tell what the end is going to be. I read their appearance on the body of a text and get its message. I see a sign which means one of these words is going to insist on being used: He's walking with a cane — probably had pneumocystis; what's that spot on his neck — Kaposi's sarcoma? He forgot what he just said — dementia? His hair has that peculiar thinness, he looks weak, pale, lost, tired, ruddy. (He looks better — taking AL721? He's gaining weight — from AZT?) Did I have a night sweat, a cough, a fever; am I weak, tired, pale, out of breath; what's that white stuff on my tongue — thrush? Am I in or out of control? I'm learning this alien vocabulary by sight — it's symbolic — but I don't understand the grammar. I can't apply it to any other situation; it's a purely local dialect. Desperate, I use these medical words as markers, to chart the distance between my body and absolute fear, or my body and the hope of health — represented as control by the command of Scientific Terminology and its promise.

We have conversations in various forms whose essence is *disclosure*. One is sero-positive or -negative, another has just been diagnosed. The buildup to announcement along a route of suspense: Sit down, I have some bad news, X got . . . , or Did your hear about . . . ; more and more minimal overtures to stage the news, down to a single dolorously inflected, "Well `. . ." (I told J about L and — as I expected — he cried hard. D said, "You got to bust his cherry.") We terrorize each other with the news, we get giddy and push our desperation toward the small comfort of The Absurd, staged as impossible excess. We take tests, and friends hold our hands as we receive the word which threatens to define us, to force us into the duty of its own replication. It's dry; the word burns out of control. His news precedes him: scent on the wind. (I'd heard about S but I hadn't seen him yet. When I did see him I asked him, "How are you feeling?" He looked at me — about to disclose his diagnosis — tilted his head quizzically — then realized because I'd asked not How *are* you but How are you *feeling,* that I already knew.) Sometimes we know things about each other we didn't want each other to know — whispers and hand-me-down disclosures — and we are even *friends*— but we know that vocabulary in the hands of others creates stigma, grows in the social body as the virus grows in the physical. "Positive" and "negative" becomes signs not just for our physiological trials but for civil restrictions, and in these matters we are rarely wrong in trusting our deepest paranoias. (On our first date, W — handsome, warm, mature, sexy — told me he had mild symptoms of ARC [AIDS-related complex]. My desire was confounded, cauterized at the source. He left feeling embarrassed and somehow guilty; I left embarrassed, guilty, and ashamed.)

And the demand to hear the voice of concern, magic words, from my — especially — "straight" friends, and to voice back, continually, to those I know are ill: How are you (feeling)? To care to ask; dare to find out. And be prepared to listen to the litany of fear, rage, loss, disease; to be an open ear, organ of sympathy. And if someone passes, be witness, give testimony, tell stories, name names. Yes, I am well, but I am surrounded by a quilt of names (The Names Project — over eight thousand commemorative panels sewn together) — a comforter — creating among a congress of the dead a community of the bereaved. First names and last names, nicknames and drag names ("We miss you girlfriend"), alongside the artifactual evocations of kinship and culture: ball gowns, leather jackets, teddy bears, rodeo boots, political buttons, snapshots, and glitter — and the interpolation of desire read as care, the carefulness with which a quilt by many hands is being stitched into a poetics of loss. This, on a panel:

His love came at me like a river. I felt so inadequate as though I were trying to catch it all in a tin cup.

God bless you Luis. May god allow me to stand before you when next you open your beautiful Spanish eyes.

***

Some are able, we have seen, to tell: to live out their evictions as full tenancy and shock us with what they understand of what we can barely see. In the midst of this all I saw my literal father die, faint expirations, fainter than any he'd ever before taken, round little puffs he blew like smoke rings from his cheeks, five or six only, lighter than air. The macho bull exited like the sweetest ballet fairy, relaxed at last, soft spoken, delicate. Some men I've seen — how do they do it? — I don't know — and only some have — live sharper, richer, after diagnosis, become bigger, more generous (and not just the context) as they become thinner and weaker, have found a calmness unsettling but calming to those around them, so fine is their strength and so little do the rest of us know about death, bereft of ritual, corpse, and interment, surrounded by our fears projected as the grotesque.

Eric was my good friend T's sometime lover; hence in proximity to my daily life if not exactly of it. We'd seen each other dozens of times over ten or so years, but had never really spent time together, just the two of us. He got sick and died slowly, the first I knew well to transform, to metamorphose along the disease's route of thin, thinner, thinnest. A possessor of erotic power most of his life, he never let go of it, by which I mean to say that his body never became an ugly thing, though he was radically disfigured. His desire to charm outpointed his powerful adversary. A small army of friends were his defenders, scheduling precisely his daily meetings, meals, sheet changes, medicines, and "dish" sessions. Eric's dying was a site of empowerment. The server and the served were connected by the line of interdependence that constitutes a meaningful act. As he got sicker, T tried to draw me into this nexus of exchange; he knew the degree of care needed, knew I could be useful, and recruited me — it was for *him* I did it, as if he were the one in need of care (as, of course, he was). I committed to feed Eric lunch on such and such a day.

I was nervous, hadn't yet confronted anyone head on who owned the disease, wanted to be correct, polite, less fearful than I was, more comfortable than I anticipated being. First we tended to functional details, then Eric and I got down to the serious business of being casual. Almost immediately, he showed me the way. "You know," he said, "one of the nice things about being sick is that I get to see the people I like, but wouldn't ordinarily spend time with." With a swift lunge of graciousness he'd assumed the position of caregiver by putting *me* at ease, making *me* feel good. By turning the occasion away from illness and towards sociability, he located himself as a giver as well as a taker — a liver instead of a dier. Eric was *living of* AIDS.

In the end — a year or so of abstract fear, a year of diagnosis — Chuck and I were great friends. This after twelve years of community association — shared podiums, rallies, cultural events, meetings; do-gooders in our mutual minds, busybodies, respecting each other but never actually — yet — friends. But something cut through as he got sicker, a relief, release, that led us together as if we'd really known each other during the twelve years we sort of had. We grew old together in a year and a half — with the shared vision of ethnic cultural kin — like East Coast Old World Jews in our Miami rockers. We laughed a lot (given the situation), criticized and critiqued, argued, and basked in the easiness of our longterm newfound alliance. How did he make me continue to feel he was cute — "a doll" — I did — even as he grew frail, emaciated, at once bony and soft — like a monkey, I said — his evaporation process seemed sweet even as I cursed it.

This is the very tiny part of the story I want to tell: M said he thought Chuck was beginning to show signs of dementia — final terror down the road of struggle when you can't even form the idea of "courage" to bear you forward — and this was a rumor that prickled all our skins. It was Thanksgiving; on my way to the country I was to drop off for Chuck some of my Turkey Day prizes: Viennese Marzipan Bars, with homemade almond cake bottoms, apricot jelly layers, and bittersweet chocolate tops. I didn't want to be feeding them to Chuck-who-wouldn't-know-where-he-was. I was scared, though I hadn't myself seen any indications to confirm the rumor — but really how many space-outs would it take to signal the onset? Ah, my doll, my girlfriend-in-arms from the old days anyway, my honest dignified teacher, as I trepidatiously entered your room that day not knowing what to expect — this weird ironic American harvest ritual — you called to me from across your bed, your boat out in a few days, with full holiday spirit called to me cheerily across the room, "Bird Girl!" By which I knew you knew it was the day of stuffed turkey, that it was a good and a horrible day, that we were "dolls" together speaking in code, and that you were a "queen" in full undemented possession of her essential ironic distance.

Then — O True Bird Girl — you flew away.

Long blond hair, flowy clothes — this was in 1974 when I met him — an impeccable sense of colors and their dream co-ordinates, handsome with real bone structure, and even literary smarts. Everyone knew, could *see*, Jackson was a renaissance man; he could do *everything* (except maybe relax) — at that time weaving hand-spun and -dyed clothing, and writing a little poetry. But *Design* would cover my sense of his power: the ability to place things in juxtaposition — objects or threads — so that their uniqueness was set into resonance — like a tuning fork — each unit or strand or line brought into active consonance with the others, a poem. I should say that when he died a year ago, after struggling with AIDS-related lymphatic cancer, and he had long since ceased to be the modelly beauty of yore — though testimony to his personal power and insight even increased (and I saw it in his person, which I couldn't name a "corpse" only hours after he died — he was strong, present — electric even — his constellation absolutely in order) — I gazed at his body floating in bed, but couldn't help noticing, also, the books on the near-by shelves — how they were *arranged*, some on their side, some standing, some leaning — in a precise balance — the objects on the side table too — and I admired, envied that order which nailed the exact image of casualness, composition, and serenity: the material world in luscious objectivist presence.

But his wound had opened — unhealed open "mouth" on his neck from a gland that hadn't quite been excised (the "mouth of hell" I thought) that he wrapped in his own famous scarves but couldn't keep closed. Once and then twice it ruptured that morning, hemorrhaged so that he could see he would be swept away in its profusion of blood. And so he asked C, his lover and primary caregiver, to carry him into the garden so he could "bleed into the earth." "Let me bleed into the earth." Jackson was able to arch over his death this worshipful poetic figure, to guide as communion a passing that others would read as being taken away. Blood streaming around him like a heroine's hair, Jackson arranged his last words, and put the world in order. Who knew that a man could have such precise integrity in that particular moment, could engage his death *actively*— with cognizance and will — as a life image, could make of his final moments not a destruction but a creative act?

***

My friends reading these drops on paper, of this, now I am sure: We can die with our hats on, we can die with our boots on, we can call ourselves by name as we enter the rolls, we can pierce the ground and draw in the dust — in the dust of ourselves! — on dissolving knees — the complex design of our presence and release.

[1988]

Further Under

Ten years later of unnamed terrors and specific losses, AIDS comes closer into my life in waves, "waves of nearness," raising its shark fin in my direction, then circling farther. The blood-scented waters could make one pass out . . .

Some, of course, do pass out — right out of the circle. But if anything besides rage is clear in these drowning surroundings, it's the clarity of those few who seem to quicken in their sickness and dying, those gifted few who stay awake as they fall away, and offer to us attendant comrades instructions from the beyond, or the going-beyond.

It may be my own voracious sentimentality and romantic yearning that seek to transform these bitter passages into something more informed. Yes, well, but I've had at least serious co-conspirators who've given me my figures, phrases, mantras, mudras, holy dish . . .

Leland was well into ten years of ardent Tibetan Buddhist studies when his first KS lesions appeared, and had already weathered crises in his new ancient faith. He'd left a live-in ashram in an attempt to localize, individualize the mind-stilling Buddhism he craved (as he'd sought even before AIDS to still a sex-crave that kept him ever hungry, in Buddhist terms a "hungry ghost"). But abstinence of flesh wasn't for him; he had a more modest — and grander — goal of achieving fleshly pleasure without gnawing the bone, of finding a serene balance right here in his quirky gay life of theater, theatricality, drama, and drama queens. So when AIDS announced its way through his body he was already troubling himself into a distinctly American — one might say San Franciscan — Buddhism.

As he began to sicken and die, he kept his eye hard on the process, informed by ritual precepts I can't repeat for being uninformed. He watched his body as if it were *a* body — *the* body — and tracked in his agitated mind the one purposeful Mind. If it sounds high minded it sounded so to Leland too: he was constantly failing. He was constantly succeeding and failing.

In between hospital visits, over a home-cooked meal, he detailed the problem to me. He was using mantras and other self-awareness exercises to quiet his thinking. "But every time I get to a certain place — a level — and think I'll be able to relax into stillness," he complained agitatedly, "I start to hear the theme from 'Bonanza' — *Bonanza!* — and can't concentrate!" He looked more than frustrated: tried, tested, chagrined. "There it is, so ridiculous. I try to dismiss it and can't relax." He saw the irony in his dilemma, but was nevertheless exasperated, stopped at the threshold — *and he was trying to die well* — by this paradigm of idiot chatter. He couldn't break through.

It seemed to me that as long as you had an idea of "breaking through" you weren't being, or accepting, where you were. But young John, cleaning Leland's kitchen, put it to him more gracefully. "If I got to that place," he shrugged, "and I heard the theme from 'Bonanza,' I'd just start singing it." His Buddhist lesson was simple: Go with it. Sing 'Bonanza'! This natural comprehension charmed Leland completely. He was humbled and thrilled and knew John was right. Was he even a little shaken such direct understanding came from someone unschooled in the lore, cracking an already shaky belief in the doctrinaire forms he'd been studying? I don't know if he actually took to singing the theme song, but that mundane media riff lodged in his mind opened a door. He began to gain the courage to transform Buddhism to his own specifics of a mid-life Hollywood-bred theater-tenured brilliant quirky awkwardly frustrated subtly flamboyant queen dying of AIDS in 1990 San Francisco.

Nesting uncomfortably in his last hospital bed, he told me of the new trouble he was having with one of his former ashram mates, who felt him straying from the Way, and was raising alarms, making him feel like a Bad Boy. Having struggled through thirty years of homo sex-guilt to find some measure of peace-of-mind-in-body, Leland found bad-Buddhism death-guilt not very attractive. Tibetan was beginning to turn him off. The ornate, symbolic Tanka paintings he'd actually helped print in America were starting to seem alien, exo-cultural. Who was Shiva to him in California; what in Sanskrit spoke to his idiosyncratic world? He wanted to die, he explained to me, governed by the things that already mattered to him, that came directly out of his life, ritualized by early investment and repetition, then fixed in the firmament for guidance. Could these even be his own *theatrical* icons, long ago installed: Elizabeth Taylor, the Trembling Bountiful, or Barbra Streisand, the swan-voiced Yearning Duck?

As he spoke his mood was growing more excited and defiant. He was coming to a vision of "grace," informed by the sublimely silly creatures of the gay quotidian, suffered, nurtured, transcended, and adored. "Barbra Streisand songs *are* my mantras," he squealed heretically. "They're what I know by heart, what I already repeat and repeat." This was too good. I glanced at the photo of Liz he'd tacked on the hospital wall. Fresh from the bath in her ripe-skinned middle period, she gazed serenely — unabashedly — from beneath a pink towel done up as a turban. All she lacked for true diva status was a jewel in the forehead. "Here's your goddess, your Kali," I said — Liz didn't blink — and we howled. Something had been transformed. The daily world one lived in had sprouted its own golden feathers. Leland had found his rhythm, and started to relax.

The next day I brought him a homemade tape of Streisand's second and third albums — the songs we both knew well — had, in fact, grown up together singing — and on which Streisand's voice still maintains jazz inflections, a girlish purity of sexual longing, and a mature woman's saturation of sexual fulfillment and loss. This time, though, the clear plastic box read, "Barbra Streisand Sings Tibetan Buddhist Chants," while on the tape itself was printed, modestly, "Babs sings Buddhism."

I'm a reporter, I see now, rereading this tale. Ten years of AIDS has altered my poetic gift, narrowed my eye, humbled my language. What do I know about death except what my friends have shown me — I let *them* speak — for what did I know before, a virgin, uninitiated, unendured? Death's literalness is what I've been given, and the poetics of struggle have forged from it not transcendence but enactment. That fact of acceptance — the acceptance of that fact! — lies before me like a series of steps, rigorous, unsentimental, hilarious, florid but precise . . .

After Leland returned home from the hospital — which he desperately wanted to do — I sat on his bed and welcomed him back. "Well, you're home, now." "Yes," he replied, "I'm home and I'm going somewhere." That process, surrounded by a vigilant circle of friends and family, brought him in and out of lucidity and strength, though never at the price of clarity. After a dip that seemed almost certainly final, he rebounded. Thin and frail and blemished, he dished through some photos with J and me. Then, in what was the last detailed conversation we had (aside from my explaining to joyous him that the life-support system was being withdrawn), Leland, with the exacting eye of a critic, and the forgiving eye of a fan, and the third overarching eye of a born director, explained to us, barely audible, rasping and gulping the words, the precise differences between Angela Lansbury's and Tyne Daly's interpretations of Rose in "Gypsy." No more fear now of having Inappropriate Mind. If "Rose's Turn" was the theme song at hand, it would be embraced. Did he *perform* it? — I can't remember — it seems to me he sang all the songs. And it seemed to me that this being-who-he-was to the end was validation for all he'd been before, indicated the peace and acceptance he'd rigorously struggled to achieve.

He died quietly the next morning. When I arrived at his house a few hours later, I peeked into his room, saw the flattened covers where I expected a mound, and was surprised that his body had already been whisked away. It seemed too soon. I talked with gathering friends. One asked if I'd gone to sit with the body. "But it isn't there; I looked; they already took it away." In fact, I was told — "But I looked!" — his body *was* still there; I glanced back through the door — where? Then I noticed, collapsed beneath the blankets as if air alone had sustained it, now exhaled, deflated, one-tenth of its former size, a few barely noticeable bumps raising the covers, the suggestion of Leland's body. The rest had vanished, puff of smoke. It was hard to believe someone had been there; it was hard to believe something was there now.
I didn't look.

The little decisions people make create the one AIDS narrative that keeps me sane. I'm made to understand the meticulous dimensions of life lived thoroughly by those in the process of losing it. Ken, gaunt and bruised, whose dying radiated power, who shared a very purposeful half-hour with me two days before he died (though I was really his lover's friend and hadn't known him intimately); sharing just enough time, I think he thought, to educate me, to let me feel his acute mind and sharp will issuing from utterly ravaged body. Ken, who thanked me for coming, and when I answered, on exit, "No, thank *you*," threw back in a clear voice, instantaneous and unaffected, accepting my acknowledgment without vanity, "You're welcome." Ken's body — which I *did* look at — hands bent backwards touching beneath his chin in a death mudra laid out by his lover, impossibly unnatural in life, winged articulate in death, his tightened face eyes wide open — having seen the Virgin Mary come to take him, flaming sword and heart — gazing up and out, open gazing, open gazing . . .

Or young John, desperately thinning, in a burst of exuberance donning a pink and turquoise sun dress, blond curly wig, sunglasses, and blue kerchief, vamping on my couch and rug like the skeleton of Nancy Reagan (but Nancy Reagan *is* the skeleton of Nancy Reagan!), utilizing both his body and his loss-of-body, exhibiting outrageously what I might call not *joie de vivre* but *joie de mourir.*

Or Ken again, emaciated in bed, booming a voice from what hidden reservoir?, in a chamber of tropical plants, chants from an unseen tape recorder wafting like smoke through the room, like wind at the door, with a clear luscious photo on the nightstand of a hidden beach, long and curvaceous. "Is that in Hawaii?" I asked. "No, it's in New Zealand, near my friends' house." I knew he loved the talismanic sea. "Have you been there?" "No," he answered carefully, "Not yet . . ."

[1991]

Orphée
The Kiss Of Death

The poet falls in love with the world and constantly dies for it
— circle of frenzy and release — *Orphée!* Or the poet expires so
that his (her) words may live [is that the same as not having a
social life?]; he falls literally into the hands of L'Amour La Mort.
Orphée (Jean Marais) and his Death (Maria Casarès) stalk each
other. Their primal attraction is poetic divination and fate, seen
in love's mirror as mutual fire-in-the-eyes. "It's not about understanding; it's about belief." Expectant, vain, exalted, Orpheus
takes his lover's vow, poet's creed: "Toujours?" "Je jure." The
rhyme of 'always' and 'I swear,' oath of eternal enactment, is the
same for artist and lover: to go *all the way* through the mirror's
veil. "Say forever."

For Cocteau the drama's a Parisian romance played out between pompadour and high heels. The scene borrows glamour
from Hollywood to push the metaphor and make it itch: The
eternal oath is sealed with a hot kiss. She's in two-piece wasp-
waist Escoffier and he's all jawline and blond raked hair. Where
earlier the radio of inspiration might have been the muse's well-
spring, now it's background music to an embrace. Casarès lights
a cigarette. "Do you love this man?" demands the judge. Casarès
exhales, says nothing. Insistent, "Do you love this man?" "Oui."
Orphée swells and gasps; Death's black gloves and pearls. Alone
in the adjacent room — "Mon amour" — they touch; they kiss.
They fall to the bed. Casarès's teardrop face — pointed chin and
radically upswept eyes like Satan herself — is bathed in light.
They lie down forever and swear.

After fifteen years and perhaps a dozen viewings, I'm watching the movie again with my students, having offered to initi-

ate them into Cocteau's mystery: the resonant unfolding charm of perfect metaphor, each side ceaselessly amplifying the other. This is the heart of the movie, the scene that's always held me in thrall, Death explaining the universal chain of command that I've read as Creative Order, the order of Form calling the poet to work: "transmitted by so many messengers that it's like the tom-toms of your African tribes, the echoes of your mountains, the wind in the leaves of your forests." But this time I'm feeling weak at the knees; something new in the scene disturbs me — I feel oddly embarrassed, *shocked.* I'm pulled out of the poetics and land in the purely transgressive nature of the kiss: unsettling, scandalous. He's kissing *death.* It may seem moody and romantic but he's *making love to death* . . .

Why am I so unbalanced now by this familiar scene? [D. H. Lawrence: "Why does the thin grey strand / Floating up from the forgotten / Cigarette between my fingers, / Why does it trouble me? // Ah, you will understand . . ."] These well-worn words have redefined themselves: kiss of death, The Kiss of Death. How altered my sense of this stock phrase, how literal its reinvention . . . How fearfully, now, behind each stolen kiss; how courageously behind each true one . . . How familiar death has become in my casual life; how complexly my friends have embraced it. Ah, you will understand . . . AIDS . . . AIDS.

For now overlaid upon Cocteau's poetic myth is a real kiss, newly fabled. My old friend Marshall is nursing his dying lover, Ken. The frame cannot be bleached of Ken's wilful blue sores, skeleton-haunted body, feverish lips. Hollywood lighting will not erase the shadow in his cheeks, ashen tinge of skin. In a pale room, on a San Francisco hill, the morning before Ken dies, his lover's oath continues: "I love you, baby." To his mother: "This is my farewell kiss to you." To Marshall, eagerly, "Kiss me, baby." Ken doesn't have the advantage of a cinched black dress and pearls. He's wearing padded hospital diapers, pulling them down because he feels they're not sexy. He says to Marshall, "Suck my lizard tongue." Marshall does.

I'm shaking in the juncture of Cocteau's spirit-zone and my friend's house. Do actual death and disease derange the vital romance of this lived "scene;" do they disgust and terrorize, black out the spotlight, stop the radio? I've seen in the announcement of this true kiss a hail of blisters, spiral rashes, white spots on the tongue, thin lusterless hair, sunken cough-wracked chests, purple swollen noses, fading eyes, parched throats. In my work, at my desk, on the tip of my pen, on your lips, on your tongue — I see Jackson's distended lymphatic neck, Eric's giant eyes, Iolo's broken walk, Chuck's pushing skull, Leland's loose-pulling skin. These are the images that would stop the kisses, silence the poem. They don't stop Marshall, who's met his fate in Ken's love, not in his death. Whose oath takes him within the failing heart of his beloved, and beats *there*. Marshall, who delivers a fearless kiss in the transfixed zone where death's permanence lets love keep living.

Before encountering *his* death, Orpheus is dead tired, his form has gone flat. Celebrity has leeched from his work the edge of daring. He *pleases*. "Orpheus . . . your most serious defect is knowing just how far one can go," but no farther. In the words transmitted from the zone by dead Cégeste and the Princess — discrete surreal phrases and the formal purity of numbers — Orpheus rediscovers his passionate disequilibrium. He pushes through to a place he doesn't understand but believes in, down through the layers and accretions of mud, language, faces in the mirror, beloved's glances, worn rhythms to an intuited measure found in a black and pure embrace.

The poet meeting his fate in poetry, the lover in loving: propriety serves neither, both must go too far. In that rapturous clasp of Orphée and his death I recognize the grip of devotion, the intent out of bounds, the pure *work*. [Robert Duncan: "Our uses are our illuminations."] Throughout the Zone — "memories of men and the ruins of their habits" — and haunting the house, mere information restrains hand and heart, the giving and the art. Many are abandoned by those unwilling to go far *enough*. "Will it be easier if I say goodbye?" asks Marshall, standing there. "Yes," answers Ken, "Say goodbye." And here the kiss of death is love's wound healed by love's avowal.

PRINCESS: I must leave you, but I swear I'll find a way for us to be united.

ORPHEUS: Say "forever."

PRINCESS: Forever.

ORPHEUS: Swear to it.

PRINCESS: I swear.

[1992]

A Lull in the Void

Postscript to "Turn Around"

I'm driving up Highway 101 north — spring fields of yellow mustard and those *positioned* cattle — toward beloved Harbin Hot Springs to burn off some work-related tensions. My Chopin (he's *mine!*) is on the tape deck, a compilation of impromptus and singularities, the last remaining Chopin unfamiliar to me. Suddenly that delicate "Berceuse" begins (its feet barely touch the ground), a few lightly swaying notes and I'm plunged — I'll be plunged forever — into Ney's dance for our friend John, dead at twenty-eight of AIDS.

My text that goes with this music (Part II of the dance, "Turn Around") addresses John through a range of endearments (*Johnny-Pie!*), inviting him to share the kind of art/events our friendship reveled in — an eclectic spread that spoke to the absolute delectation of cultural education, and had as its undertow — big sister to little sister — the Passing of the Lore: because I'm an official Old Queen now (I subscribe to the opera) and he was a baby one (a taste for Debussy preceded by a devotion to Barbra Streisand). I thought I had completed a gesture (I thought Ney had completed a gesture), but hearing "Berceuse" today brings John's death back with a vengeance. We spin in circles to maintain equilibrium. (Ney swirls Part III of the dance in a centrifugal white skirt.)

Norma said lately I've been looking good, *seeming* good. I attribute this new sheen to purposeful employment and to what I'm calling a lull in the void: nobody close to me has died recently. It's a small grace, and fragile; it can turn around. This man John who was really a boy to me, who was so young to me, little brother or little sister, this Johnny-Pie is last year's passing. (It was several months after writing Part II that I found out 'berceuse' means 'lullaby.')

93

Death is so *open!* My writing's unequal to the task of bringing John back to life (his contradictions alone were too breathtaking!) but his dying returns to me, regularly, a restless farewell loop . . . There's a movement Ney does over Chopin's music — you should see it. It's tiny, a lateral sway, a shuffle to the side like a blown leaf. It's what I was listening for today . . . a little music to rest the dead . . . or *lullaby* in the void . . .

[1993]

My Memorial

Either the temple itself is rising — how can such massive stone columns float in the air? — or you are descending beneath the floor's bared lip, the massive floor's meter-thick lip, to an underground (underworld?) stone chamber, airless, where a man stands as if already crushed by the ceiling's weight. "The fatal stone" is set. In the deeper shadows a whisper, a rustle, alerts the man to another's presence, a partner with whom to sing "*il nostro inno di morte*": "our hymn of death." Their voices unbounding pressure in duet will brace the stone, and turn their death house into a resonance chamber.

But you're not watching a Metropolitan Opera broadcast of *Aida*. You're here to listen to Aprile Millo and Placido Domingo (especially Aprile) sing for me. "*O terra, addio; addio, vale di pianti*": "Oh, earth, farewell; farewell, vale of tears." Aprile will throw her Egypt-blackened face skyward — to where the sky beyond the tomb-top *would* be — and spin her voice into a silver thread — attenuated to that point where matter must become spirit — as she sees "our wandering souls fly to the light of eternal day" : "*volano al raggio dell'eterno dì.*" "Ours" in this case is hers and mine. I have died of AIDS. And this is my memorial.

Listen ceremonially to some of the music that has *meant* me — a scrapbook requiem of ever-elaborated enthusiasms, polyphonic collage. As Immense Ptah, "supreme creator," is invoked by the priestesses, the temple seems to be lowering — for the tomb must be entombed — and the final note is an Italian plea for peace, "*pace!*" Already that silvery purified note of "*al raggio*": "the light" has escaped its mortal prison: We're singing to you from beyond the grave. ["Remember me," pleads Dido in Purcell's opera, "but ah! forget my fate;" and I keep misremembering and hear "but *don't* forget my fate.]

Ecstatic transubstantiations in song recall my fate — but wait! OK, I'm an opera queen, a drama queen, a melody queen, a moody thing (a "Thrilling Thing," says Genet), and the gay DNA in my hypothalamus or wherever has dutifully progressed me from aria to lieder, but I don't (evidently) have HIV and I haven't (yet) died. But listening and listing — splayed on the sofa — I compose my sources: as the speakers play, as the speakers *speak*, they textualize parts of a funeral service calling backward over me. There's self-dramatization worthy of a comic book queer, here, but the grand guignol theatrics are played out on a thrusting stage larger than my small foyer. What transpires on it is multiple, choral, and the recital is repeated in terrible modulations. Light the honey-glow candles in the wall sconce (gilded oat sheaves) and sharpen your antennae toward the tufted San Francisco night. Falling notes breeze in and out of beveled-glass windows, apartment to apartment, receiver to receiver . . .

I *have* held Leland's leaf-weight hand as the blood-feeding tubes were disconnected; I wiped Johnny's morphine-hallucinating forehead as if to clear away the false images (though it was his sister who changed his diapers); I read aloud as Chuck's dropsied brain finished my sentences with sleep; I whispered in Ken's bone-bare ear the responses that meant he could still be heard (though it was Marshall who changed his diapers). And from time to (too many) time I've gathered in company, ritually, to remember these and other loved men. Death's proximity. Death's daily life. As I couch myself, listening to music ["I loafe and invite my soul . . .", Whitman], I fabricate, inescapably, the tenor and texture of my own memorial. The solar-plexal moans and muscle chords of Bach's unaccompanied Cello Suites, or the harmonic inhalations of Chopin's Ballade #1, rupturing into cascades that flood the lungs as if a chest might really open into wings . . . I've attended memorials made of such deeply coded catharsis.

There's a tape you could borrow; written on its side with a blue felt pen is "Honeybear's Memorial." It contains the music Marshall assembled for his lover Ken, and the cassette box details Yoko Ono's plaintive "Beautiful Boy"; K. D. Lang wailing "So In Love"; Kiri Te Kanawa as Schubert's "Gretchen at the Spinning Wheel" (ah, *Clotho, Lachesis, Atropos*); Montserrat Caballé, from a rare live Nov. 24, 1970, recording, unveiling Bellini's aria "*Dopo l'oscuro nembo*": "After the dark cloud," a crackling record surrounding Caballé's beneficent soprano with ambient noise, ticks, coughs, the walls themselves demonstrably reverberating and so responding; and Elisabeth Schwarzkopf ("through want and joy we have / walked hand in hand") singing the last of Strauss's "Four Last Songs" ("At Dusk"), where the supernatural Strauss tones and planetary orchestrations disperse into even rarer constellations ("around us the valleys fold up, / already the air grows dark") as the orbital soprano seems to unite with expanded space. Interspersed with Rilke and Whitman poems, this memorial "concert" is for Ken by Marshall, and reveals the precision of a high queen's high sentimentality, and the excess of a florid lover's furious love. "*Dass wir uns nicht verirren / in dieser Einsamkeit*": "We must not go astray / in this solitude." . . . After the music we climbed Tank Hill to spread seeds of California wildflowers, as elsewhere I have tossed fistfuls of body-ash mixed with the seeds of forget-me-nots . . . We were sowing *Johnny* then, and at *his* memorial we had listened to . . .

Is it an endless threnody, then, that rehearses itself in my candle-lit house? A *melo*drama where the music ("*melos*") has returned to claim the stage. Not my own valediction, but this ceremonialization proper: the power of art to encode affection itself. *The living eager attaching eros.* "Of that softest hair" (Elly Ameling sings Obradors's "*Del cabello más sutil*") "which you wear in braids / I must make a chain/ to draw you to my side . . ." In the music/poetic that I'm hearing, human desire is enacted in the creative strain and release of phonemes or blue notes — and these enactments, in turn, become the *objects* of desire. We adore as we listen and read; our adorations lodge. This is the charm I imagine at work cast upon Rachmaninov crescendos or Reynaldo Hahn's modulated smoke: *I* can be found there! [Whitman: "Now it is you, compact, visible, realizing my poems, seeking me . . ."]

This retrospection we might share is now engaged. A loved-one's loves are lived again in the favored words or songs that we attend. "I should like, my darling, to be a jug in your house," sings Elly as Obradors, "to kiss your lips / when you went to drink": "*para besarte en la boca, / cuando fueras a besar.*" Or be released as music toward your elegiac ears. Generous act of your attendance upon my own attention.

Listen: Remember me.

[1994]

Some Haunting

"He is a ghost, a shadow now, the wind by
Elsinore's rocks or what you will, the sea's
voice, a voice heard only in the heart of him
who is the substance of his shadow . . ."
— James Joyce, *Ulysses*

If he's sitting there now, it's transparently — *literally* so — and
I know he may whiff and re-congeal in another street, another
café. Most of the time he (*they*) will be seen from the back, or
glimpsed, peripherally, in passing; when I come home I'll tell
David, "I hallucinated Kenny today," or, "I hallucinated John."

I'm no longer afraid these AIDS apparitions might be real
(they've lost the advantage of surprise), but my subsequent
clench at the gut or failing of the knees shows a terror more
truculent than fear of the Impossible. (The Impossible? What,
any more, is that?) These particular visitations — these "voices
heard in the heart of him" — pursue. They know my name, and
my whole shaken body responds to their address.

The ghosts who walk in my city (my ghostly city) are cast as
vividly as any childhood stored in a dipped *madeleine* — with that
fleeting precision memory affords, and the rubbed-out edges it
requires. And they rise just as suddenly. But their appearances
are oddly interdependent, communal. They haunt *bodies* rather
than places. Born as adults in affectional mutuality — exchanged
caresses and comradely struggles — my reappeared friends remain so framed, and show their faces by traversing planes of living faces: faces overlaying faces. Their anxious, drifting outlines
cross and merge with passing strangers — strangers filled with
similar resonating passions, and hungers large enough to invite
in, whole, another's presence. They flash and seize.

During these concentric crossings (I theorize) "Jackson" or
"Jose" reanimate toward me, pulse for a passing moment through

99

a flesh they once informed. Alert to the scents of shifting desires that surround them, they tremble, eyes open, through the familiar winds of social heat and social rapport. Shining eyes catch eyes; mine by their corners.

These visions are gone in the next shift of wind, of course — shift of a mouth or shoulder that reroutes the familiar image to the unfamiliar: just somebody else. Too late, for me, who have been stuck by recognition, a *madeleine*-rush of memory that comes, alas, too frequently to be savored, but whose measure is too steady to be ignored.

I am haunted.

***

Like many friends I've lost many friends to AIDS, a range of relations from intimate to "anonymous," but of them all one's incessant return puzzles me: why young John? Other friendships were dearer, others longer lived. Yet in peripheral San Francisco his appearances, quicksilver, are inescapable: on a bicycle there in mud-green knickers, at the café with overstuffed art-bag slung, cruising the park with a fresh buzz cut and a goat in his gait. I haven't consciously, nostalgically looked for him; didn't *choose* to seek him out above the rest. But — rushed overlays, multiple facets of a shifting center, various frame — I'm surrounded.

It's wise Yolande explains the fact I might have known had my knees held: you *don't* choose. The ghost chooses *you!* My daily wants and needs aren't the occasion of these hauntings. Each ghost has a hunger come to me for his own fulfillment. John hungriest of all, at twenty-eight his torn-out-of-youth death leaving live threads flailing. His compositional eye and draughtsman's hand just begun to merge common power in photography. John, whose innate interrogative restlessness allowed him to distance *and* devour; ravaging and scavenging through art forms, art histories, art communities, affinities, oppositions, to make a map his skillful unlearned feet could walk on . . . Torqued by the desperate agility of his gymnast's body he dwindled, as he grew, simultaneously, older *and* younger: an apparitional old man in padded baby diapers. John, who documented his bodily demise in a series of dispassionately precise photographs,

[It's hard enough to be shamelessly naked in this body-despising culture, but to be so in a sick body when the same culture paradoxically and faddishly valorizes health takes fearlessness. That the sickness in this case is the dreaded and misunderstood AIDS makes John Davis's straightforward gaze even fiercer. Void of guilt or shame, without seeking pity: these photos do not concede. They insist on being figure studies in which a human body seeks articulation. From a leeched 97 pounds to a fluid-swollen 120, John Davis remains a figurative artist, not a disfigured one. The skeleton, the musculature, the skin and eyes: these are the working elements of a photographer/model who catches light and disposes of it formally. The courage to seek such transformations in spite of systemic pain is the heart of Davis's power. The grace of his willfulness matches it pose for pose.
　　　— A.S., for an exhibition, 5/92

John B. Davis leaves us with an outline that is an in-line: the phenomenon of his skeleton's arabesque. This unsentimental view is a gift of mortal presence, one man's self inscription, an alphabet of being. His fearlessness is awakening, and might make us each attend our own hand's particularity. AIDS brought him to this attention, in despite of its ravages. He outlasts it.
　　　— A.S., for an exhibition, 11/93]

and so fused his questions into observations *we* observe, the body's palpable inquiry extended ad infinitum.

Extended beyond those old, fixed borders, to where the gates slide easily, admitting and exiting. If he walks, as ghosts do, if he walks with me now — feeding, searching, feeding: since his very mark was *hunger* he must still be hungry! Caught fleeting and reflected in shards his raw unfinished purpose stalks the crowded streets of my city, "signaling to be opened." Haunting me it seeks completion.

How do I serve this dead young man?

[1994]

Inscribing AIDS

A Reflexive Poetics

The terror, that coming-to-get-you shark with its boom-ba boom-ba boom-ba beat, the already gotten, and the disappeared . . . or (seen from above, perhaps) the valiant, the ceaselessly experienced, the made wise, and the transcendent — all those I might truly call the authors of AIDS — for years I watched and watched myself waiting, unverbalized, unwritten. Pressed upon, the writing task's new complexity (it might have been simplicity) bound me with awkward restless unaccustomed silence.

The idealism evident in my early poetry, which sprang from post-Stonewall enthusiasms and maintained the heady pansocial syncretic critique at large in the "underground," was already floundering under pressures from both sides: a diminishing value in gay liberation theory from the visionary to what I call — votable — the civil-libertarian, and the formal challenges agitating poetry from semiotics and linguistics. By the time, early 1980s, AIDS began to claim unavoidably my most attention, the poem was emerging as explorative maneuver, and the idea of thematized writing had become problematic.

My naively confident self in whom ideologies provisionally cohered as rhetoric was cracking (or expanding), like theory's subjectivity under attack and multiple-fracturing, thousand-eyes. A poetics of inquiry and ellipsis was being privileged over one of declaration and intent. But the rupturing emergence of the epidemic ready to impale one looked monolithic from any view — hideous cyclopean frontality — and in what form could writing usefully address its brutal presence?

I saw two possible utterances relating to AIDS and its government watchdogs: Shit! and Shoot'em! The one, of loss, seemed to me woefully personal, an interjection wilder and more desperate than communication, maybe even sublexical; the other, of rage, was being dynamically expressed by Act Up, Queer Nation, and a host of ingenious community-indigenous organizations and I didn't see how — poetically? — to add to that.

But one may neither make meaning, as I'd thought, nor find it, after pursuit. Meaning may be delivered — bouquet or bomb — head on. For a writer, this is experienced as a demand. How to write AIDS named me.

There was no longer any way around it, only multiform ways into it. A thematic writing, then, and if so in what way, given poetry's multifocal shifting attention? I thought that "essay," narrativized as witness and textured by interrogation and digression, might hold the sought-for argument or analysis that poetry kept elliptical. A monolith is not elliptical. The pure rampage of facts unleashed by the disease demanded scrutiny, the heartbreaking lure of incessant efflorescing information — to turn mortal details beneath the scoping light of sentences, to penetrate them, to release them, to be released from them. [Whitman: "As they emit themselves facts are showered over with light."]

So these nonfiction writings enmesh personal narrative and literary critical methodology, discovering that in the holistic dimension of AIDS each seemingly independent or oblique avenue leads inevitably to the viral core. Here, the procedures and vocabulary of art fuse with those of daily life — the biography of events — to demonstrate the impermissibility of such a separation under these aggressive circumstances.

I saw how theater, as dance performance with text, utilized the tensions of direct speech in a way the page couldn't, the electric tension of face-to-face confrontation and the body's tangible stresses. I wrote for dancer Ney Fonseca a piece in which the offstage voice — it may be the voice of the virus itself in its incarnation as Fate — demands that Ney encounter it — dialogic — in his own body. I'd required the dancer, HIV positive, to confront choreographically elements of his own mortality, and that encounter was the dramatic nexus of the piece. Ney was given the choice to take this on or not — he'd have to experience it each time behind a very thin screen of performance — and I knew I could merely offer him an opportunity written at the edge of propriety, threshold of permission. The risk I only wrote was one he'd have to risk.

Qualifying assent. Nonfiction writers know this scribal process better than poets who enact the Imaginative as the Real. I've passed my AIDS writings among their living sources to help determine accuracy. AIDS reality has enacted my imagination.

Poetry found its way, first as compound metaphor, then structurally. "The Depositories" and "Strips and Streamers," finding kinship in scenarios of war, estrange and reconstitute Whitman's Civil War vocabulary, pushing images of battle and comradely witness to a newly disoriented wailing point. In "Human Immune," the speaking subject inhabits experience from simultaneous locations as if all persons of voice (first, second, and third) are equally at risk. The poem proceeds formally via an epidemiological model: each "stanza" inexorably increases in length by one line, an expanding vortex. Hell is round, the motif, revealed to me at the reservoir point after being awakened from a weeping dream-cry, may bear Dante's centripetal impasse, but also dimensionalizes AIDS from the personal to the historical: the curve one rounds is also around one, surrounding, a world. For the gay community, this circumnavigate descent can be read as the procession of history itself disappearing. *"Chi é costui che sanza morte / va per lo regno de la morta gente?"* "Who is this that without death goes through the kingdom of the dead?"

To characterize this visceral struggle as esthetic is to recognize an ecology of paradigms, a streaming mutuality of influences artistic and social, and to pay attention — poetics — as if one's life depended on it.

Where the relational body and the medical body use the same skin, the metaphoric implications of AIDS seem inseparable from the literal ones. A recent spontaneous mantra, passing through my regular walks in the park, announces casually, "AIDS has destroyed my life." Though presumptively antibody negative, to what extent is this a poetic figure, and who will chart the distinctions? The rising sentence has no emotional affect as it tests itself on my tongue, except the startled recognition of its effortlessly clean transmission. I blink and scour the hillside.

The gnarly pines are there, and the tiny green plums, and Mt. Diablo fudged by the haze.

   The matters of fact are materials. Among the interdependent life of forms characterizing human experience and the mutable various life of form we recognize as poetry, the Human Immunodeficiency Virus is also a form of life. Unchosen, unsought, it, too, inscribes a cellular plan, like the DNA code itself is said to inscribe a measure of destiny. Interactive, its dogged contentions are inescapably creative. HIV transforms, even at body's remove. The complexity of its microscopic purity rages outward. It's writing me.

[1995]

Shifting Paradise

To shewe yow the wey, in this viage,
Of thilke parfit glorious pilgrymage
That highte Jerusalem celestial
   — Chaucer, *The Canterbury Tales*

I finally framed the painting by Tasha Robbins — an abstracted cross-swirl of tree stumps, raising among its energy loops a curious reminiscence of human figuration — and the portraits and posters on my old familiar walls, having duly shifted places to accommodate this newcomer, are calling to each other (to me) with reawakened vigor, as if by being moved they've fallen under new spotlights, baring their active souls again for my renewable eyes. Chairs, end tables, moody lamps, regularly do this dance in my house, and over again what's seemed fixed loosens, reshapes interior meaning as complementary presence, pluralized out from each object or piece of art to bear relation in a cosmology of household deities.

Here on the cheap lightweight foldout bookcase — it pretends to Japanese — under the orange volcanic vase spewing trails of eucalyptus nuts and corkscrew willows — is the one personal photo that owns a public space in my art-stuffed apartment. Five young men caught mid gambol in a park, a little chorus line of kicks, gropes, arm-over-shoulder wraps, and wide too-wide smiles. Yes, that's me (if you don't ask I'll point it out) in the wild-prophet hair and beard, a tangle of exuberant energy far the other side of saturation. My tucked-in cotton kimono's bared to the waist, where you can spot — look closely — the much-admired hand-beaded belt (snakeskin-waffled in maroon, mauve, and chalky blue) with its moon slice mother-of-pearl buckle. The ferocity of hair and pure glaze of sunlight reek of period. The year is 1975 (it's forever 1975!), the men are queer (well, one is "honorary"), and Golden Gate Park has offered its swooping cypresses and Monterey pines to border the rolling fields of that summer's Gay Freedom Day celebration.

There is no other picture, in my house, of paradise (though there is a "vale of soulmaking"). Whatever reconstellating takes place, its rarified image stays true. The spontaneous fraternal beatitude, renegade eros, and radical hilarity of that San Francisco hover, like elements of celestial Jerusalem, at the apex of memory; no maturity, no fine mellowness, no deepened work dissolves them. Through the clear painterly air — as if all of San Francisco had northern light — epochal details sharpen. There, the city's edge-of-the-world history joins its urgent Pacific geography to clasp my hand in a lover's vow (I married San Francisco on a brisk craggy hilltop in 1978, in lieu of a boyfriend.) "This other-Eden, demi Paradise," rhapsodizes John of Gaunt, similarly England-besotted, "This happy breed of men, this little world, / This precious stone set in the silver sea."

Extravagant phrases of praises gild memory — one no longer knows the actual from the iconic — the icon becomes the actual! Where physical distance blurs temporal distance refines. This much has not shifted: on a shelf a lucite frame encodes the past in a photo — unregenerate — as a paradise of pure loss.

But something has shifted: the resonant image, gingerly holding its chemical colors against the fading powers of sunlight, remains the same, but the very nature of paradise has changed. Even while — eyes dewy — focused back on primal beauty, the unforeseen — HIV — transfigures sight, beholder and beheld. "This sceptered isle," Shakespeare's Gaunt has said, "This fortress built by Nature for herself / Against infection." The magic island is flooded in a breakaway recursive tide; what did not hold — infected — returns to alter the image of origin. [Stein: "Let me recite what history teaches. History teaches."]

We stage the past in jeweled terms — to fix its daunting fluidity and give name to our nostalgia — but HIV has modified this delicate taxonomy. The paradigm shifts. A newly burnished glaze shines. A viral invasion has reconfigured the utopian body, so that what once was seen tenderly as "youth" is now revisited as the unacknowledged genius of "health."

The circling age rings in Tasha's painted tree trunks, I see today, are like the ovoid loops we practice to draw the human face.
Her small oil of a foot among clouds rises, on my bedroom wall,
above Nikki's green collage with its palm-forward open hand.
Familiar domestic talismans, these — one sleeping, the other
awake — that make of any wall a window through which I view
some measure of self. Catching the last flare of sunset, they signal it across the room to a poster, in French, for Fellini's *Les Nu-
its de Cabiria*, where Giulietta Masina, in a chicken-feather coat,
flutters her fingers gamely at other seekers winging the night.
In this crosswind of salutations the photo from 1975 has moved
to my work table. Under gooseneck light I study its captive lumi-
nosity: its fable of youth, to be sure, and florid sunny conviviality,
but more, now — shifted paradise — its depiction, its retention,
of life before AIDS.

[1995]

July

You look for summer in repeatable signs, different from preced-
ing and subsequent days but identical to other summers, as if in
concentric loops you enter again the same zone with the same
apprehensible attributes: that dust smell of the dry weed field
by the river, the pancake of heat, or these swollen roses puffed
on the dining room table, creaming pale magenta, lavender,
and pink in a moiré pattern, fading color into color the way silk
does, seizing light and inhabiting the shine from within. And,
too, repeatable, here at the annual Fourth of July picnic, the
talk has turned to weather, as over the palomino Sonoma hills
stream the first incursions of a coming sky-wide fog.

On a low brick garden wall I pull at my turkey burger, eyeing
suspiciously the shredded carrots embedded, as Steven nudges
his marinated off-the-cob corn. Last week the heat was bone Cre-
tan, we say, but this imminent chill at the pool party is really
the way summer seems to be heading. It's OK to talk about the
weather after twenty years of casual friendship. We're all familiar
here, even those of us who don't know each other, familial, safe.
We show our aging bodies in the sun shamelessly, shorts or swim
suits, shirts or not, because at this point our physical changes,
as communal as they are inevitable, are endearing, and if we
comment we compliment each other, not because we're liars
but because we appreciate — and distinguish — the difficulties.
["You are astonishing, you look as young as ever," the Duchesse
de Guermantes tells Proust the narrator, and he moans to himself, "another melancholy remark, which can only mean that in
fact, if not in appearance, we have grown old."] But to us even
our moderate age is, we know, a rarity in plague time; which of
us will get to be old? This information passes among the passing

clouds and passing sun. A barbecue is trying to nail down summer. Steven and I are laughing. Hamburger juice dribbles. From the corner of my eye I see, halfway down his calf — I hadn't known — the bright purple flower of a KS lesion.

Zalman has built a new pool; its consecration is the official business of this year's party. The pool is lovely, but the enclosure is dramatic: a white graduated stucco wall with a capping of Spanish brick hides the pool from the suburban house, and tilts the brief ascent toward Hollywood — a white terry robe could slide down your shoulders before you reach the water. In the center of the wall glass blocks turn the sunlight aqueous, and, from poolview, place us among the lapping waves of a domestic aquarium. The water is too warm, but it suits the too-threatening sky, whose heat, we see, will be short lived. A handsome man I don't know who I resisted flirting with is talking to Richard. At the end of a watery ear trumpet I hear him explaining, "The doctor wanted me to go on an IV drip just in case."

I slip on my huaraches and stay in my wet trunks — they're new — and wander from pool to patio to kitchen, sampling the garbanzo and eggplant dips (but not the tofu) and suckling a beer. I find out the two young boys I was watching play in the water with such complete rolling body contact [little Seryozha squirms in Anna Karenina's lap so he can touch her body to his body in as many ways as possible] that I thought, delighted, their early friendship was a paradigm of homoeroticism, are brothers and not buddies, and I wonder why their physicality now seems less sensual, as if the genetic/social sanction makes their touching unfelt. (I don't tell this to the mother.)

As usual, at parties, I'm drifting from group to grouplet, sampling conversation (but not the tofu). In the kitchen a trace scent of marijuana sparks my interest, "Do I smell something?" No answer, so I repeat it (that smell creates desire!). Marie must explain to Richard, who has the pipe, that I've asked for a hit, since I'm next to his bad ear, deaf from an AIDS infection. He lights the pipe, coming alive with his good ear, and we brighten together; the others, I believe, drift away. We drift in place.

"How are you . . . ?" (The disequilibrated ear has had him dangerously ill, poisoning his bloodstream. I tell him that a ringing in my mother's ear during menopause brought her close to breakdown, though others saw it as "just a little ringing.") ". . . You seem better." He avows he is feeling better, details some doctory stuff I lose in the smoke, and adds: "I've been seeing a healer — a body and a spiritual healer — who said I should get ready for the final phase. He said to prepare for death by preparing my friends to let go of me." For a loving man, I see, the shape of egress is correspondingly generous: he'll relinquish life by urging his loved ones to relax their hungry love that quickens him. This is posed as casual chat; the kitchen still has six desserts on the side table, the stools we sit on are these four-legged beechwood stools. Focused, we hug.

Conversational groups re-form and I return to the fog-shredded light. It is not repeatable summer. ["I heard someone say that he quite looked his age, and I was astonished to observe on his face some of those signs" — Proust — "which are indeed characteristic of men who are old. Then I understood that this was because he was in fact old and that adolescents who survive for a sufficient number of years are the material out of which life makes old men."] Gene — a dentist and a superb chef — has cooked a glistening tart, so that the bright cherries on top are completely rounded, globular, bursting, and we joke that he must have, after baking, injected them with a dental syringe to replump them. Its perfection makes this cherry pie a sign for cherry pie. The artifice of it we recognize as drag; flour, butter, sugar, fruit in drag as a *tarte aux cerises*.

Fleeting disguise — the present constantly remakes itself, re-masks itself, shifting. The present only stands for the present. I write this, now, on my computer, to bring to completion a book about AIDS, and it's the first piece written to be in the book. I've been rereading, you've noticed, part of *Remembrance of Things Past*, and it's being reread because I find I'm in it. I'm writing now on a log in the sun in the park and I'm back at my gray marble desk (it used to be a partition in a men's room), attempting to end a book whose original title was *Breathing Holes* — gasping up from under the ice to air — but has become, you will have read, *Unbound*.

Proust's crepuscular Baron de Charlus begins a litany:

111

Hannibal de Bréauté, dead! Antoine de Mouchy, dead! Charles Swann, dead! Adalbert de Montmorency, dead! Boson de Talleyrand, dead! Sosthène de Doudeauville, dead!

and my sepulchral rhymes beat instantly: Jackson Allen, dead! Charles Solomon, dead! John Davis, dead! Leland Moss, dead! as I recognize, circumnavigating, a repeatable unrepeatable necrology.

I creep into the living room to take off my still-wet trunks, almost smoked dry by the barbecue. Richard is asleep on the sofa, his long pale body soft like a child. I skinny into my green shorts quietly, not to waken him. Robert waves goodbye through the plate glass window and blows a kiss. There's some blackberry cobbler I haven't yet tried which I keep empurpled in my mind until I'm back in the kitchen eating it. Though long cooled, its deep mushy richness gives the flavor of warmth.

[1995]

112

Generation

The storm that raged through San Francisco late in the night of December 12, 1995, shook this whole building earthquake style, and made a fragile raft of my bed, resting near the bay window that bucked and banged in the wind. The branches outside shrieked — I could see them whipping in the street's yellow light — and I woke and slept to repeated roaring gusts. The wind tore deep at the earth as if it wanted to get in: a thousand trees uprooted or broken in Golden Gate Park, hundreds elsewhere pulled out by their hair and lying with great clods of dirt yanked out with them, neatly serrated empty circles of shade on the ground. Gashed branches dangled everywhere; roads were blocked; the city whose trees are reaching maturity together woke to a loss that was generational: not once in a lifetime but a unified swath of lifetime lost.

My apartment could have been sliced in two by the gigantic Eucalyptus — "one of my sentinels" — across the way (a few blocks east two such aged hundred-footers crashed — into the park, as it happened, so the facing houses escaped.) But the radical size of these toppled beings was compelling; you never see them horizontally where their enormity can be measured human-scale. They were at once desperately, environmentally, evolutionarily sad, like beached whales, and gawkingly thrilling: A hundred years was lost, but the integrity with which their falling rewrote the landscape drew me to their monumental sides again and again to gape. I looked at the now-erect rootwork — multitudinous intentionality, groping — almost shamefully visible; I measured myself against the tank-like trunks which had smashed through other trees in their way, forming new tangles and bushworks of leaves, bark, and gouged-up soil. (The sound they must have made I'm glad I didn't hear.) The speed and scale of the devastation excited me even as I mourned the losses: so big I couldn't blink away the incontrovertible facts. I wanted the hugeness and the solidity of the mess, the grim external confirmation, the proud physicality literally shaken to its roots.

You can hear the metaphor forming as it forms, description snaking downward to sink its own "ductile anchors" and prop itself up toward meaning. But I had already written, AIDS-wise: "fallen giant, empty stump" three years before these winds came wailing. In the search for accountability called mortality things expand as they contract — language, too — and "to evoke an image," as Robert Duncan says, "is to receive a sign, to bring into human language a word or a phrase of the great language in which the universe itself is written."

A fierce mutability swings us between faces of the storm.

***

In a different park — though raked by the same winds — two other fallen trees initially called me to write. A pair of massive cypresses, tenuously gripping the sandy slope in better days, have thudded down, entangling the hillside. In this park, known for its various wildness, birds relish the sudden cover: Sparrows flitter among the new-formed thickets, jays scramble, hummingbirds chortle and dive. Something fruitful has happened for them, finer and richer than any recent attempts at cultivation. For two months now I've examined the uprooted scene. Here where extravagant growth is the rule the damage seemed more easily poetic: It was comfortably, I might say conformingly, pretty. The exposed rootlets bared their fine membranes in the sun; the torn wood reddened, grass grew in the upended soil collected in the furrows of the trunks. I, too, perch here, watching the spotted hawks devour the skyline.

This little park was famously — famously! — known for casual sex, though it's been drastically pruned by AIDS, by which I mean not only that its practitioners have dwindled, but that the censors and jurists early on tried to garden away the underbrush that offered pagan cover to public acts. Though its mandated legacy to the city is untamed growth, it's managed to undergo "erosion control" in exactly those spots most lavishly used. Still, it has a flavor, and no other park foregrounds its vegetation so generously.

It has been summer in the middle of February, as sometimes happens; the air thickened, plum blossoms blew out, the sky widened. San Francisco asked to be seen. I sat on one of the fallen trunks — new branch for me! — and turned my face to the sun. The heat was saturating, liquid. I felt myself expand in the hot light, nourished.

A man I knew minimally — we never really spoke — approached and kept my eyes. I've seen him for fifteen years along a variety of erotic routes. He paused to talk about the weather — you do that in San Francisco because you like to show off your luck at living here — and eyed the tumble of branches, the inviting trouble they'd made. He thought there might be human cover there too, and chuckled at the fortuitous change. The place is ghosted — we both knew that — it was nice to contemplate a turn. "It's good to see you," he said pointedly, far more direct than either of us expected, "I mean there's so few of us left. It's good to see you still around," by which he meant "alive."

It was grass growing on top of the dying trunk that originally drew my pen, preposterous and fertile like Whitman once saw it: "And now it seems to me the beautiful uncut hair of graves. //Tenderly will I use you curling grass, / It may be you transpire from the breasts of young men." I pushed the ruin of the storm to mean the ruin I needed. What constitutes a memorial, a legacy? Where do the bodies go I don't see go — no graves, no burning ghats — and how do they reseed a city lost to loss? (Instead of usual age-group percentages, the papers announced this week that AIDS was the leading cause of death in San Francisco, period.) I'll try to hold within my words the secrets of the sect, to reveal them in tight bouquets and thickets, in spectacular decay, a generation, a sprinkling and a rampage, I'll try to sew in you unshakably — no possible storm — the vitality whose vital signs were and are and have been palpable love.

"Then silence / is as silence was / again," says Robert Creeley. "That risk / is all there is."

The famous San Francisco sun has turned to famous rain. A reminiscent wind has whipped up, strewing the gleaming street with papers and leaves, anything that rises. I imagine a series of substitutions which stand for flight: black crow, broomstick, milkweed, vapor trail, pterodactyl, red balloon, oak pollen, helicopter, luna moth, dust mote, box kite, June bug, rocket man, gazelle. The wind takes them all.

[1996]

Unbound *Sources*

Jean Cocteau, *Orphée [Orpheus]*, André Paulvé and Les Films du Palais-Royal, 1950.

Robert Creeley ["Then silence / is as silence was,"], "Waiting," *Words*, Charles Scribner's Sons, 1967.

Dante [*"Chi é costui che sanza morte"*], *Inferno*, Canto VIII.

Robert Duncan ["Our uses are our illuminations,"] *The H.D. Book*, edited by Michael Boughn and Victor Coleman, University of California Press, 2011.

D. H. Lawrence ["Why does the thin grey strand,"] "Sorrow," *Selected Poems*, The Viking Press, 1961.

Fernando Obradors, "del cabello más sutil," Elly Ameling, *Serenata*, Phillips.

Marcel Proust, *A Remembrance of Things Past*, trans. C.K. Scott Moncrieff, Vintage Books, 1982.

William Shakespeare ["This sceptred isle,"] *Richard II*, Act 2, Scene 1

Aaron Shurin, "City of Men," *A's Dream*, O Books, 1989.

Aaron Shurin, "Turn Around" with Ney Fonseca, first performed for Juntos Dance, Theatre Artaud, October 1992.

Gertrude Stein ["Let me recite what history teaches,"] "If I Told Him: A Completed Portrait of Picasso," *Look at Me Now and Here I Am*, Penguin Books, 1971.

Richard Strauss, "Four Last Songs," Elizabeth Schwarzkopf, George Szell conductor, EMI Classics.

Giusseppe Verdi, *Aida*, Act IV, Scene 2, Metropolitan Opera Orchestra and Chorus, with Aprile Millo and Placido Domingo, 1991.

Walt Whitman, *Leaves Of Grass, Comprehensive Reader's Edition*, W.W. Norton & Co., 1965.

III.

III

After Genet

Jean Genet 1910–1986

Not the thing itself but the thing not itself.

It would have to start, of course, with a funeral procession out of *Our Lady of the Flowers*, where the great queens in gender exile parade their lamentations in the rain, here literarily transformed so that Mimosa I [Flaubert], Mimosa II [Baudelaire], Mimosa the half IV [Rimbaud], First Communion [Proust], Angela [Gide], Milord [Cocteau], Castagnette [Sartre], and Regine [Beckett] — "a still long litany of creatures who are glittering names" — wail with a plastic stress of language verging on black magic incantation to raise his dumpling face into its preordained saintly niche.

The monument in Père-Lachaise will be etched with the outline of his erect cock — a sign in no danger of losing its reference — or the word "cock" for a signature, which would bloom in proximity to his name, for in Genet language is always verging into gesture, golem-sensual, masturbatory, reifying itself into a stroke-able solidity, useful, purposeful, imprisoned.

> Until their warm sperm, spurting high, maps out on the sky
> a milky way where other constellations which I can read take
> shape: the constellation of the Sailor, the Boxer, the Cyclist . . .
> Thus a new map of the heavens is outlined on the wall . . .

Yet his language, too, is unstable; words as gateways from the present, opening at either end into memory or fantasy, more for exit than entrance, inconstant, hiding behind themselves to protect their hinges, escapist, riding linguistic drift in the sway of slang, the impermanent high of street lingo and nicknames that in the mouths of his characters are not so much signs as markers of a way, meaning, frequently, the opposite of what they say. "I am forced to use words that are weighed down with precise ideas, but I shall try to lighten them with expressions that are trivial, empty, hollow, and invisible." And containing, also, the knowledge that language is a caste system, various private and semi-public networks, rigidified by class, race, and gender; so fiercely identified they have near biological power:

> Slang was for men. It was the male tongue . . . it became a secondary sexual attribute. It was like the colored plumage of male birds, like the multi-colored silk garments which are the prerogative of the warriors of the tribe. It was the crest and spurs.

He is not outside his noisome Christian dialectic, who, like Baudelaire, can only use the oppositional negative terms in hopes of detoxifying the state-sanctioned positive ones. But his bitter graces bring a whole new people into church; the canonical force of his writing not only sanctifies the criminal, the mad, the Queer; it throws the popes and judges into the shit-pile. (Though he will, of course, transform the shithouse into a holy confessional.) A young man at the café complained (having seen Fassbinder's *Querelle*) of its negativity. He's post Gay Liberation longing for positive imagery, felt Genet's abases and dooms are debased and doomed. But the same aggressive Christian dualities are still used for political disenfranchisement, and their terms still need to be turned around: *immorality* (by which the Meese Commission may wind up banning Genet as obscene), *disease* (by which the Justice Department and Gov. Deukmejian sanction discrimination against people with AIDS), and anti-scriptural *illegality* (by which the U.S. Supreme court gives the go-ahead to states to declare private consensual sodomy illegal). I understand the desire for confrontational imagery that's nevertheless positive (not to mention freed from dualistic terminology altogether) but given, say, Reagan's familiar penchant for deliberately misusing oppositional terms (the deathmaker missile as Peacekeeper, the CIA puppet Contras as Freedomfighters), Genet's insistence that "negatives" be "positive" is still helpful. And his awareness of how the State appropriates the Church's moral prerogatives to create criminals, though it landed him in prison, also helped free him from it, turning the tables to earn for himself Sartre's sobriquet, "Saint."

. . . and the insistence always that sex and gender are political controls, socializations rather than biological imperatives, "I will speak to you about Divine, mixing masculine and feminine as my mood dictates." Who more clearly tells of the renegade power of queens, their strength of purpose, their negotiation of humiliation into pride, without forgetting to detail the holes from being on the firing line, the piece-out-the-side that masculist culture inevitably carves for itself? At the same time they (he) are locked into adoration of the masculine, they deconstruct its terms, make fun of it, rename it, dress it up, and *then* go down on it. For pleasure is the mode that both canonizes and deflates masculinity. And in Genet full arousal is achieved only when gender is subverted, when the man posing as masculine meets the man posing as feminine. The paradigm: Our Lady, the murderer, goes to the ball in a silk dress, dazzling. (The bar is called "The Tabernacle.")

They enter the brilliant fireworks of silk and muslin flounces which cannot fight clear of the smoke. They dance the smoke. They smoke the music. They drink from mouth to mouth. Our Lady is acclaimed by his pals. He had not realized that his firm buttocks would draw the cloth so tight. He doesn't give a damn that they see he has a hard-on, but not to such a point, in front of the fellows. He would like to hide. He turns to Gorgui and, slightly pink, shows him his bulging dress, muttering: "Say, Seck, let me ditch that."
He barely snickers. His eyes seem moist, and Gorgui does not know whether he is kidding or annoyed; then, the Negro takes the murderer by the shoulders, hugs him, clasps him, locks between his mighty thighs the jutting horn that is raising the silk, and carries him on his heart in waltzes and tangoes which will last till dawn.

Behind a veritable smokescreen that diffuses the usually sharp boundaries of gender, Genet brings his characters together, their meeting point the immovable phallus veiled with the moveable dress. *Then* it plunges into masculine thighs. Genet's penis has a foreskin of silk that mediates its meetings with men. Traditional signs of the feminine drape the traditional signs of the masculine, in the service of a sexuality that *uses* them both. Subversion of gender is *not* the subversion of pleasure. My queen-friend, back in the pre-safe-sex days, was screwing an anonymous male, who in his throes turned around and coo'd, "Fuck me, girl." . . . and they danced till dawn.

How a subculture learns that language is indeed a creative constitutive force, and how that force generates and degenerates behavior. "Divine was metamorphosed into one of those monsters that are painted on walls — chimera or griffins — for a customer, in spite of himself, murmured a magic word as he thought of her: 'Homoseckshual.'" So they learn to sabotage its terms, affronting its reverences as they rename themselves. Humor, revealing self-awareness, takes the sting out of contemptuous categorizations. There is no natural stance, there are only poses. No real face, only masks. Names call forth ritual presences — especially cross-gender names, since gender-aligned names are already ritual delimiters —

> When the name was in the room, it came to pass that the murderer, abashed, opened up, and there sprang forth, like a Glory, from his pitiable fragments, an altar on which there lay, in the roses, a woman of light and flesh.

Feelings are the gestures of feelings, a self-reflexive semiology: "I'm the Quite-Alone." "I'm the Quite-Persecuted." "I'm the Quite-Profligate." "I'm the Consumed-with-Affliction." The article (the) qualifies each stand as a dramatic stance; language, gesture, and dress combine into a costumed drama of social forces intimating selves. "Madame née Secret." Genet evolved a narrative where fantasy and memory mold time to their urgencies; where the moment itself cannot be transfixed, no reality unequivocally defined, where language is contemptuous of singular meanings and characters exfoliate identities. "It is customary to come in drag, dressed as ourselves."

[1986]

Note

All quotations are from *Our Lady of the Flowers*, translated by Bernard Frechtman, Grove Press, 1963.

Smoke

Take a nice bourgeois society, screw it tight with corruption, manners, sanctimonious religion, and suppressed eros — all in the grand French style; what comes out is the irrepressible truth: Jean Genet. Instead of niceties read criminal behavior, instead of manners the transformation of genteel gender by dragqueens, instead of religion a profound meditation on the powers of darkness, instead of sexual repression read sexual spew.

In his great novels (*Our Lady of the Flowers, Querelle, Funeral Rites, The Thief's Journal, Miracle of the Rose*) and plays (*The Balcony, The Screens, The Maids, The Blacks, Deathwatch*), Genet drew a picture of the twentieth century's underbelly, a world hidden from light but swarming with vitality. From inside France's most infamous prisons he reinvented romance and law. His heroes were queens (the *original* Divine), murderers, soldiers and sailors, madames and whores. He saw in sex, violence, and even gender disarray a political revolutionary force. What's more, he spun these figures from his imagination in an electric language that charged them with seductive power.

In Genet's world, it's the nine-to-fivers who are repellant, the judges who swim in hypocrisy and shame. Hello Jesse Helms. The movies made from his writings do not always have the same vigor as the originals, but in their characters and relationships they retain the clarity of his assault on social taboos. Under the gun of a new wave of censorship and intimidation as we are, it's helpful to see our tormentors so clinically exposed, to revitalize our own struggle with the breathless vision of homoerotics he offers.

Genet does have his eternal moment of the screen: *Un Chant d'Amour*. In the supercharged hotbox of prison, radical tenderness flowers. (We knew that from our own lives.) When one prisoner passes his lifebreath of cigarette smoke through a hole in the wall along the length of a straw to his friend, it contains the beauty of every secret exchange, glance, letter, or touch passed from man to man or woman to woman through the ages of heterosocial domination. And honey, nobody — not even Bette Davis — has ever, before or since, smoked on screen like that!

[1990]

Synching In Tongues

Lypsinka is pure limelight, sculptured by artifice and sustained by illusion. She is the postmodernist's maxim come to life: nothing is real, everything is represented. From the moment she arrives on stage to the tinny burst of canned applause, Lypsinka assures us things are only what they seem. This diva reinvents drag for the 1990s by showing that gender and showbiz — the twin domains of the transvestite art — are equatable. They are both constructed by gesture.

A series of obscure, wacked-out musical numbers provides the plot for an evening's entertainment. With her elastic mug and balletic upper torso, Lypsinka overstates every word, bringing each nuance to its rightful inevitable climax. Nothing can be too broad in her world of fabulous phoniness. Every song ends with the triumphant stance, legs apart, arms thrown up into the lights, mouth open in complete fulfillment.

Drawing on her glorious notorious tradition — Charles Pierce to Craig Russell via the Cockettes, the Angels of Light, Sluts a Go-Go et al., Ethyl Eichelberger and Charles Ludlam, plus every dime-bar queen with a thirst for affection and a flash of understanding that gender is essentially theatrics — Lypsinka perfects the notion by imitating no one, by being imitation itself. The trick of lip-synching in the gay community has always been that it used the mask of voice (its seeming authenticity) against the mask of the body (its seeming authenticity). That clash gave queens what amounted to a private genre in which to practice their public arts, with entertainment as the final mask for defiance.

But Lypsinka's drag persona refers to no one but herself, not Diana, not Liza, not Judy. She purposefully draws from arcane Broadway tradition to find singers we *don't* know, emptying the impersonations of reference. Her performance doesn't get clouded by how "real" she's doing somebody. Lypsinka is freed from reality. When she shimmies and shakes and snakes, she is the pure will to be fabulous.

The music is hilarious, and the mix is inspired, from a freaky unsettling devout jazz rendition of "Getting to Know You" to such corkers as "I'm a Bad, Bad, Bad, Bad Woman (but I'm good company)." The range stays pretty close to a low Broadway/supper club repertoire (though a hideous Osmonds version of "Yo-Yo" elbows in), and the diva whips through it all like Mame on martinis, elegantly in the know and unerringly over the edge. At times the tape mix pulls her through its changes, twirling her around like a witch commanded by her own spells, changing tempo and voices, synching in tongues. Her tour de force is a frantic succession of ringing phones, each answered in the voice of another scorned, desperate, righteous, attitudinal woman — mostly snippets taken from vintage movies. Lypsinka races across the stage, lifting the imaginary receivers, mouthing the lines, both caller and answerer, driver and driven. Again theatrical and transvestite arts merge: we are inhabited by multiple bodies, multiple voices, multiple selves.

She can't do the schlock gay anthems "I Gotta Be Me" and "I Am What I Am," because they're too limiting. Lypsinka understands that identity is about plurality, and her musical appropriations and verbal collage are a triumph of permission over containment. When she plants her long legs and sucks up the spotlight, you know she's gonna blow. Anything might come through her, a vessel for the demonic *and* sublime. When she sings, "There'll be some changes made," she means it. She rolls her permanently arched eyes, thrusts a swan's hand to the heavens, and draws down the powers that be. Nothing is real, everything is permitted.

[1991]

At the Pulling of Invisible Strings

On John Wieners's "A Poem for Trapped Things"

One that has been not just lovely but useful for me . . . How JW lives out his broken-sweethearted fairy persona, dignifies it . . . That act that makes coming out a declaration of faith, spoken amidst the bullshit and fears toward an intuition of possible beauty. That you're broken, "trapped," is not yours but the social, especially JW's time, but that you speak your *longing* is individual indomitable volition and vision. Broken, maybe, but also broken *through.*

"A Poem for Trapped Things," its subversion of distress by wonder. I read, inevitably, fairy wings into the butterfly, Wieners's "red robe" if he'd get up and spread it. How much, for me, the content is mutated by a homosexual iconography. "A giant fan on the back of / a beetle," indeed, our scurrying, squashable, defensive personae lifted ("with the enormous bale / of their desire") by incessant dreaming a calling to dangerous love wings out of us, closet-y carapace completely belied by coy and fluttering fan. The valiant/manqué female Hollywood images, beloved of gay men in search of viable animas, sparkle here in subtext: "we could / vanish from sight like the puff / off an invisible cigarette" lit, no doubt, by Paul Henreid and passed to Bette Davis, nobly toasting their fading romance with the intermingling of their smoky sighs, the coordinated heaves of their inhale/exhalations; or "blue diamonds" à la Monroe proving their value only in relation to MM's yeasty vulnerability. I'm yanking out the subtext in vocabulary from its lyric concordance because that helps locate for me a JW facing his soul as butterfly I think I recognize, know. Could it be beside the point that I first encountered this poem around 1970, at an initial meeting of what was to become the Good Gay Poets in Boston, read by Charley Shively to those of us come, after all, to pursue our pursuit of the poem in a place where we could comfortably spread our wings? It's a natural: our coming out, like dingy caterpillar, from cocoon of fear of eros into *display*, the lure, command, and dazzle of sexual delight. There's humility in JW's encounter, the self before the glorious other, but also somehow that we don't just see it, we *be* it.

[1985]

Note

John Wieners, "A Poem for Trapped Things," *Selected Poems 1958–1984*, Black Sparrow Press, 1986.

The Gaze of Julie

In the theater of drag — as in the new theater of movies — the camera is the legitimizer of artifice. A drag queen is a star playing for the vaselined lens. I show these drag photos to my friends to document my illusion. The photograph is manipulated *before* it is taken.

The arrested performance in snapshot is happiest there, thrilled by incontrovertibility, at rest among its array of gestures threatening to over- or underdo. The transvestite art incarnates into a fixed set of gender signs (costume) a fluid range of semiological poses (attitude) — where the fluidity offers the one danger for the facade to crack, reveal its underpinnings of large pores, stubble, jawline, shoulder, bicep, adam's apple, or poor thin hips. The truly accomplished queen is she-who-moves, who arrives throughout, not just in select flashlit moments. Dear camera, at least frame me among those lesser lights, with your truth-telling history and my Houdini gaze.

When I found this Cleopatra cum Lulu wig, I found I could do something I'd never before achieved: I could pass. (Don't underestimate the power of a wig as a framing device — it is *total!*) And when you pass — oh thrill — you are doing a *serious* critical maneuver — talk about deconstructing gender — you are thoroughly mixing up the signals, fooling so-called nature, threatening that vicious system of punishment and rewards. Cross dressing and passing let me enact proof of the social construction of gender. With camera as co-conspirator I can stick it in everyone's eye.

The photo records the staged piece: black wig, pink linen jacket, mod tunic, strap-bondage heels, geometric bracelet, geometric earrings, sloping knees, gyroscopic hips, articulated hand, strawberry lips, wide eyes, blue-frosted lids. A domestic genie, in her hallway, at home. She does not look like me; I only faintly resemble her.

Dear camera, I am using your reputation for authenticity so I won't have to *say* a word, and if you lie my lie is bigger and uses yours. I tame you because my body is fiercer, my truth is uglier, my revelation more beautiful, my vulnerability more terrible and precise. Poor modest camera — thank you — you can't see the shadow beneath the pancake, the hair under the pantyhose, my dick squinched and airless, the swagger beneath my sway.

After the squealing performance, when the photo opportunity has gelled in a few four by sixes, I arm myself and start showing, at café, office, and school. I use the photos as supplementary fire, to pursue guerilla warfare into the safe belly of casual discourse. "Wanna see some pictures?" is the only introduction. So the first contact is with the full force of the sign set, a "female."

I love to show these photos to straight men — especially since the picture is of a quote unquote beautiful, even sexy, woman. Then I am The Scrambler of Desire, and I hope the repercussions are problematic. I don't have to suggest anything, the picture signals for itself. (I merely add my best Mona Lisa smile.)

Last year, though, I outwitted myself, sent another shot as a holiday card to friends, sometimes without return address and signed, "luv, Julie." For some it was merely the confusion of "Who is Julie?", no joke. I passed too well, had only my own secret charge. The naive photo just presents a gender image; it's not critical, doesn't contain commentary. For it to work, the context of the photo must include me as male — either as signatory or direct deliverer. (I prefer the latter, because it's an active wink.) The photo is my mirror, but the sightline must travel from one to the other.

The price of such hilarity is gender boredom after the fact. I'm not as big a queen as I could (ought to?) be. Ah, sweet masculine privilege, and how much easier to scramble other people's desire! But I have a little album, culled over the years — arrows in a quiver — and as long as gender reigns they remain hot to handle. As I cradle my images of self as other, I shake my invisible wig, let its smooth curves snake into my body and relax it. I believe I am looking at photographs of a woman. Then I believe I have no idea what a man or woman actually is. Fascist swampthing! Beloved infidel! Gorgeous simulacra!

[1991]

Fig. 3. Julie

Real Questions

On Robert Glück's Elements
of a Coffee Service

"One morning I was walking Lily around 29th and Sanchez" begins Robert Glück in *Elements of a Coffee Service* [reprinted as *Elements*], a disarming scene setting, like those of certain dreams, into which the wrenching urges of our psyches plunge with pure violence, upsetting our neatly ordered flowerpots. And Bob's dog-walking idyll is brief — he looks too long and too lovingly at an attractive man in a pickup truck (the kind of subtle glance only a true homophobe can catch with the awakened and sore antennae of his sexual fears) and soon that man and his companions are chasing Bob and Lily "yelling 'faggot' and 'fucking faggot.'" This scene is not a dream, though in the perversity of our parlance we'd call it a "living nightmare"; it's a possible event lifted from any one of our actual lives. Within the first paragraph of his book, Bob Glück has us on the run, and in the heat of that desperate situation he primes and prods us to question how we got there, and how we might get out.

The very strategy of questioning the reader is at the heart of Gluck's urgency in his work; in it he has found a technique that lifts apart the crossed threads of our complex social and political lives without resorting to moral authoritarianism or political fundamentalism. His questions allow both intimacy and reprimand but don't arouse our defenses — the knots he seeks to unravel are his own as well. Our answers are manifold, and they must be so entirely local that each of us may phrase them in his or her own language — but the right questions will lead us toward them, and that is one of the gifts of Bob Glück's art.

"And what I resolved was this," he tells us at the end of his fag-bashing story,

> that I would gear my writing to tell you about incidents like the one at Sanchez and Day, to put them to you as real questions that need answers, and that the questions, along with my understanding and my practice, would grow more energetic and precise.

Which they do in the course of the eight stories that comprise *Elements of a Coffee Service*, confronting our masks with the thinness of our masks' dimensions, our habits with the smallness of our habits' maps. But look: our habits and masks, our full neurotic panoply and socialized display, are enormously inventive, and Glück recognizes this. If he is trying to dispel the illusion of bourgeois safety in its familiar incarnation as food, he will *create* the illusion first, with the delight of a medieval monk cataloguing the sins of the flesh:

> What if he takes us to his villa and merely to pluck at my nipples he feeds me olives pickled in caraway, dormice dipped in honey and rolled in poppy seed, sausages, orioles seasoned with pepper, capons and sow bellies, blood pudding, Egyptian and Syrian dates, veal, little cakes, grapes, pickled beets, Spanish wine and hot honey . . .

If he *is* describing the luxuries of the flesh, to analyze their parameters, to discover what's actual and what's fictional in sexuality itself where power has erotic charge and historical determinism its own whispered language, he approaches the task with the relish of a careful gourmand:

> We stood in the dark kitchen kissing; that got old. He wanted to sit on my lap. I was so aroused I was wide open. We mutual masturbated like that and kissed. I was gasping. I caught our reflection in the window and it was funny to see us so localized inside these grand sensations of pleasure, my hips and muscles permanently cocked.

That framing device — the reflective window — is crucial to Glück's intentions; he engages us, enraptures us, and then pulls back to show us caught in the act. It's something like Castañeda's Don Juan (urging him to break habits of seeing and "stop the world") meeting the cinema's vocabulary of close-up and long-shot; describing that interface where the continuous "I," the unquestioned subject, meets its *context*, that complex of social, economic, and linguistic forces that shape so many of our choices.

But no strategies, not even a heart in the right place, will explain the thrill of the good writing here, the measured weights and balances of sentences, the interweaving of events in narrative, the way intentionality as humor can turn language inside out and yield its interior meanings (and Glück is part of a tradition of Jewish comedian rooted all the way back to Talmudic wit), or that poetic precision that is met by the reader's recognition/revelation: "It's true that I carry in my spine, wrists and knees the glance of a man I passed three years ago walking up 18th Street, and the shock I felt on seeing that he was completely to my taste."

There's an eager sleuth's delight in the unpuzzling of behavioral codes reminiscent of Barthes; a funky joie de vivre like Frank O'Hara's; and the insight into manners and morals of a medieval fabulist. The sets are delightfully and then uncomfortably familiar — following through Glück's lines of perspective requires change.

The lure of the engagement is its discreteness, its verisimilitude and sensual recognition. Are those the trappings of a trap? — if so, it fits. An awakening *demands* the loss of complacency. We read this book at our own expense, and that is literature's true reward.

[1983]

Note

Robert Glück, *Elements of a Coffee Service*, Four Seasons Foundation, 1983, reprinted as *Elements*, Ithuriel's Spear, 2013.

Reclaiming Eden

On Robert Duncan's Faust Foutu

For Robert Duncan, whose poetry searches through order and disorder for primary forms and eternal voices, Faust is a natural. From Christopher Marlowe through Goethe, Dr. Faust has come to represent man *in search of,* probing and bargaining his way through mortality to find the heart of human pleasure. Reprinted after twenty-five years, Duncan's "comic masque" *Faust Foutu* is his reworking of the theme.

Duncan resembles the Doctor in learning and dreaming; his own poetry soars and swoops and tempts the sun with the "highness" of its language, the complexity of its reference. Knowing this, Duncan challenges himself by making Faust an artist, not a scholar. He's a painter who struggles with ideas of creation as if his own body were a canvas seeking to be transformed by the imagination.

This isn't a play, Duncan makes clear; it's a masque. A mixed-media form perfected in the Renaissance, the masque marries poetry, song, dance, and pageantry in a discourse of ideas rather than a dramatic enactment. Since Duncan's language has plasticity and sensuality, the form permits its presence: the words' sonorities become the action. And let down on the ropes of comedy and song from the higher ether it usually inhabits, his language here has a delicious variety. As usual (Duncan has often emphasized that he is a "derivative" poet, in the positive sense of utilizing his sources) the poetry breathes overtones: daffy Gilbert and Sullivan twists and puns, misreadings worthy of *A Midsummer Night's Dream,* rhythmic riffs from Edith Sitwell's "Façade," refrains and snippets of children's tales.

I'm married to a Master
who is painting every day.
He has mastered his medium
so now he is permitted, so now he is permitted
since he will not go astray
so now he is permitted to play!

Duncan's playful work is not as well known as his more complex poetry, but it's an essential strain nevertheless. His Stein imitations, songs, and general wordplay are integral to his hermetic language that engages powers as well as phrases, and finds in its puns Freudian resources of meaning and magic.

Seriousness is there alongside play, as Faust pushes against walls he feels must hide secrets of meaning. "All this I desire. For this I secretly sell my soul. To conquer time, to go farther, to enter the lights." It's not possible to recount the plot — there's not one, really. It's a voyage with markers, some of which we see and hear. Faust seeks to engage life at a level of *actuality*, so that his body and its lusts may become fundamentals of experience rather than sins. "When the meaning of the play is clear we will reclaim Eden and abandon shame!" So he pushes his painting toward plasticity and his body toward pleasure. Everywhere, the human body comes forward to assert its being, a fact intended to swallow guilt whole.

Dear Human Body, ruthless arbiter. Even in rage I address you. In all your shifting guises, male and female seductions. Eternal fisher of men. In your ripe bosom, lustrous pear-clear breasts, abundant, or in your pectoral splendors with nipples like young grapes amid the hairy leaves of the vine. Eternal museum of our desire. My burning face, my trembling hands exalt you!

The hero of this play is Faust "foutu" — quite literally fucked. This may indicate the mess he's in, but is also highlights the fact that there's only one way to be born into the world. Duncan's crazy quilt of characters test their urges. As Marguerite says, "To let all chaste thot fall away, returning to the carnal dining place, the tousled bed, the few hungers and pleasures that make us more than saints."

Since poetry and drama's post-Elizabethan split, poets' plays have occupied a special but privatized ground. There are rich contributions from modern poets: Charles Olson, Frank O'Hara, Diane di Prima, and Michael McClure all utilized the genre. But Duncan's play carries a special kick for San Franciscans. It was publicly read at the in/famous Six Gallery on Fillmore Street in 1955, with a cast calculated to induce nostalgia if not longing among current writers: Duncan himself, the painter Jess Collins, the poet Jack Spicer, filmmaker Larry Jordan, and poet/balladeer Helen Adam, among others. McClure's notes on the book's back recall the edge of the times, and remind us that the era was enlivened by painters (Rothko, Pollock, Still) whose struggles and attendant devils mirror Faust's own.

This is something like the Year of Duncan, having seen the publication of his long-awaited *Ground Work: Before the War* and his collection of prose, *Fictive Certainties*. *Faust Foutu* broadens the territory, refreshes it. At the play's end, Duncan seeks to un-spell his magic. He's not a laurel-rester and never has been comfortable with endings, this poet whose major ongoing work is entitled "Passages." He seeks to bare his purposes, reveal his motives and his essence. As he faces the audience he disrobes.

> Now. Look at me! This is me, torso. Hairy as never was a god, the animal sleeps in its dirty hair like a fire in a nest, a rat rooting with greed in garbage. This is me, Side-Show. This is none of you. Over the beautifully weak shoulders that might have been, had I served them, thrilling to the avid devourers of strength in the body, over the soft round tense nervous ashamed exposed shoulders the animal hair, that cares nothing for *me*, spreads its apish splendor . . . As I speak I am trembling as you hear me tremble because I am exposed. I am only me as you see me.

At a reading in 1981 at 544 Natoma Performance Gallery, Duncan performed selections from *Faust Foutu*. As he reached this closing speech, he followed his own command. To the audible gasp of a startled crowd, he slowly, tremblingly, unlayered himself. His sixty-year nakedness had won for him a shock-of-the-new no youth could buy: an image of The Real. In a quavering voice he faced the crowd.

Alive with shame so that living through shame I may claim my
place among movie stars. I may retrieve my immortal image
from all perfection. It is *my* torso that strikes wonder so that
the gods are dismayd.

It was a human act.

[1986]

Note

Robert Duncan, *Faust Foutu*, Station Hill Press, 1985.

A Restoration

On Beverly Dahlen's The Egyptian Poems

Measures figure in the imagery, the feather that weighs the soul, *words in the balance*, but also the figure of measure itself, a felt solemnity in the *pace* of syllables, announced immediately as *Ah Ah Ah Ah Ah pointing to the mouth* so that a ceremonial order of breathing and speaking organizes the poems. That fundamental "Ah" — nasalized as the first cry or open as the last gasp, inarticulate as a stutter or all-meaning in the "Aum" — voice of the soul in its outwards stream is emblematic of this sequence, *The Egyptian Poems*, where "mouth" is the core of generation and transformation, eating and naming in initial acts of composition: word/world.

> The dead are our gods. We must pry open their mouths.
> They cannot live without our sustenance.
> We bring hammers and chisels.
> We crack their throats.
> Our words fly open above our heads
> . . .
>   Take into the darkness of your mouth
> this eye. It will be enough light.
> . . .
>   And the great train of gods
> was called out of the darkness
> of his mouth.
> . . .
>   that my mouth is whole,
> my hands are raised, that I come praising the light.

True to its stately measure, a processional, the feet of the poem are stone, hieroglyphs, and the left to right pictorial movement reads inevitably as a journey, life to death and back, *I have come so far / I have made this journey.* So the Egyptian method of writing, imagist par excellence, fuses with the verses' natural movement. And the gods appear in their place as proper persons of the poem: Osiris, Thoth, Shu. For Dahlen there are also father and mother — her themes are generation and relation. *See my mother gathering in the darkness* is also Dahlen as poet "gathering meaning" — the Indo-European "leg" in "logos" means "to gather" — and so she is, inescapably, Isis piecing the limbs of her brother together, *See how my father's head has been restored to him. / See how his wounded mouth has been healed.*

A Gnostic shadow names life the wound that is born by the initial separation, a void or emptiness whose air we breathe. Dahlen moves toward death (her father's?) for healing, for *restoration*. Generation moves forward and backward in time, in and out of realms, *The dead are our children . . . The dead are our gods . . . The gods are our children.* We move in and among each other as souls set free of genetic order into an interdependent and interchangeable roll. Names hold the key, *Who are the gods*, the act of naming, *His name becomes us / when we die*, knowledge coming-into-being, *This is that god who / came to himself and knew his own name.*

Am I being elliptical? — you bet. I am pussyfooting around a stone measure as if my feet were afraid of getting caught in the tracks. The pronouns of this poetic sequence are ill defined so as to be addictive: you could fall right in place, be *the first one before you / the last one behind you,* and I would not say whether you want to or not, but would say not lightly. *The name of the god is hidden.* I would say authentic as a sacred text the word "hieroglyph" implies. Printed on papyrus- and parchment-reminiscent paper so as to make you tremble. Could a book be too pretty? I was afraid of sullying it with my hands. In short, treat it with respect.

[1983]

Note

Beverly Dahlen, *The Egyptian Poems*, Hipparchia Press, 1983.

Reading/Writing
An Introduction to Derivations

There are books inside of The book, and readings within Reading: for Robert Duncan all small books participated in the telling of the universal Book, and Reading was the means by which — small or large — universal design, coherence, first principles (and their contraries) made themselves manifest to human consciousness. "To evoke an image is to receive a sign," he says in the *H.D. Book*,

> to bring into human language a word or a phrase of the great language in which the universe itself is written. Here, to experience is to read . . . It is the belief that meaning is not given to the world about us but derived from the world about us, that our human language is a ground in which we participate in the cosmic language. Living is reading the message or poem that creation is about.[1]

As he read from and wrote in this world book, Duncan developed a poetics at once contemporary and traditional, a disturbed poetics inhabited by regulators and invaders, the disjunct and the designed; a collage of elements among whose various tensions the cooperation of balance between parts and whole that constitutes reading was enacted — a poetics, he reminds us,

> in which the poem is thought of as a process of participation in a reality larger than my own—the reality of man's experience in the terms of language and literature — a community of meanings and forms in which my work would be at once derivative and creative. [2]

142

In this experience of living he called "reading," the powers of language in their zones — literatures and their histories — were constitutive forces like physical laws or biological imperatives, where "books are as real to me as mountains and trees and bushes."[3] *Derivations*, then — one of Duncan's key terms — proposed an open field of literature which does not refer to experience but *is* experience, a mode through which we receive and transmit primary sensory, informational data — as we might breathe in sunlit air, or shiver in the rain. As with Blake's "the Authors are in eternity," and Pound's "all ages are contemporaneous," Duncan's "derivations" indicates a continually cross-pollinating universe where "the contemporary opens upon eternity in the interpretation of times,"[4] and in which participation we are conjoined and cohabit. The body mirrors — no, *is* — the body of a text whose thriving is reading, and each poem lives as a cell among the larger orders of Poetry. "So I have written and rewrite I am a derivative poet . . . even as I know my physical body and life-pattern to be derived from the common code and the dance of two strands of encoding."[5] This process of derivations is a distribution of meaning among constituent parts, each merging and emerging through "self" and "community."

> When I experience on the other hand in my extreme persuasion to the reality of the world created by the written and read words, where the meaning in language has its definitions in the community of meanings from which I derive whatever meanings I can, is at the same time a feeling that there is no real me, only the process of derivations in which I have my existence.[6]

Such spiritual rhetoric certainly has its sources in Duncan's theosophical upbringing, where all experience was read as being revelatory of hidden meaning. But Duncan grounded his poetics in a practice that made compositional principles from these hermetic orders, "this body of words the medium of this spirit." So with his homages and translations, his collagist design, his use of rhyme, and his insistence on the polysemous nature of poetic language, he concretized reincarnationist and world-soul dicta.

Duncan's colloquy with other writers forms a major part of his written work; he took "community" to actively mean writers — living or dead — he was reading, as well as those — living — with whom he was — well, arguing. This work includes three long series deriving directly from Stein, "Imitations of Gertrude Stein 1951–1952," "Writing Writing," and "Imitations of Gertrude Stein 1953–1955"; two books of *Dante Etudes*; the translated "Chimeras of Gérard de Nerval"; "Poems from the Margins of Thom Gunn's *Moly*;" "A Seventeenth Century Suite in Homage to the Metaphysical Genius in English Poetry" based on Raleigh, Southwell, Herbert, Jonson, and John Norris; "Circulations on the Song" after Rumi; poems addressed to and concerned with Lorca, Pound, Zukofsky, Levertov, H.D., Spicer, and Blaser; poems based on phrases from Ovid, Shelley, Milton, Blake, Pindar, Baudelaire, Verlaine and Wagner, and Celan; and his ongoing life-work, the *H.D. Book*. As such, "derivations" indicate a discursive poetics, going back and forth among texts and their writers, as if all participated together in the formulations of form, and the coming-into-being of literary meaning. "For in writing," he says,

I came to be concerned not with poems in themselves but with the life of poems as part of the evolving and continuing work of a poetry I could never complete—a poetry that has begun long before I was born and that extended beyond my work in it.[7]

In the proposition of collage Duncan found his means of permission, a structure for the live operation of derivations, a vulnerable yet tensile openness to influence. His "Passages," in the range of their fields, absorb and constellate a variety of linguistic material as influx: quotations and foreign languages, unascribed and untranslated, enter as discrete presences — retaining the signals of their otherness — and yet contributing to the overall design and coherency. "The great art of our time," he says, "is the collagist's art, to bring all things into new complexes of meaning."[8]

Similarly, rhyme proposes kinship of linguistic units with each other, individual phonemes or syllables entering through memory into time, calling forward and backward, pulling at discrete reference for a larger coherence in structure, and awakening the ear to vibrational affinities in the storehouse of language sounds. And "a word does not rime with one word only but with the population of words in the language of poetry."[9] So *uses*, as well as sounds, constitute rhymes in the history of literature, and "derivations" proposes textual, as well as sonic, rhyme.

Collage, as structure, and rhyme, as operation, are *polysemous*. The artist after Dante, says Duncan,

> works with all parts of the poem as *polysemous*, taking each thing of the composition as generative of meaning, a response to and a contribution to the building form. The old doctrine of correspondence is enlarged and furtherd in a new process of responses, parts belonging to the architecture not only by the fittings . . . but by the resonances in the time of the whole in the reader's mind . . . Every particular is an immediate happening of meaning at large; every present activity in the poem redistributes future as well as past events.[10]

These populations of rhyme, assemblages of quotations, libraries or texts, and resonances of meaning parallel the workings of community, as the individual feeds and is fed by social forces, creates and is created by the various public and semipublic languages brought to bear. Duncan's most inviolate nature, his working dialectical relations with peers; Olson, Spicer, Blaser, Levertov; his ferocious correspondence; his purposeful teaching at Black Mountain and New College; revealed his insistence that poetry be actively interrelative — supported by the poet's active relations. "The poet," he paraphrased Whitman, "was not individual in his genius, for that genius was the genius of the people; the poet in his poetry an awakening in one of the poetic intent of the mass."[11] And, elsewhere,

> I would not have taken the task had I not come at last to feel <u>calld</u> to its order. I am the writer of a Quest. When I speak of the poet's intention that must govern the text, I speak of an entity of the Imagination that what I most truly am serves. In the poet's intentions, I am calld to my fullest responsibility, to my responsibility for a community of poets that I have come

to in the commune of Poetry itself. Not an abstract idea but an actual ground of actual poems and of a communal content.[12]

In chapter one of the *H.D. Book*, Duncan describes the specific terms of his being called to order. It is the story of his early life as a reader, and it is, significantly, as a reader that he comes into the fullness of his calling as a writer. It was around 1937, he tells us, on the Berkeley campus, couched on a lawn with two friends, reading aloud from Joyce's *Collected Poems*. With the two women as his audience and chorus, feeding each other's imagination of literary depths and possibilities, they were, he says, "trying the scene and ourselves to find the plot and our role there." Suddenly the campanile bells rang, calling out the academic orders of classes and examinations, while lower classmen streamed toward the gym to perform war-preparatory military drills. "I have to go."

> "You don't have to go," Lilli commanded, raising her hand . . . "Stay with Joyce." What we had been enacting, the reader and the listeners—the muses, perhaps, for some serious amusement or enchantment was worked through our cooperation—celebrating this most high reading of the poem, was to become real. "Rejoice with Joyce," Athalie commanded. A poem was to take over.

Between the sanctioned orders of the academy and state and the magic orders of the poem — attended by his guides — Duncan poised . . . and then read on. "Away from me the disconsolate students went as I read. It was too late. I could never make it. I would be late. Without an excuse. This poem of Joyce's was not an excuse; it was an affronting fact. The time was gone."

But *that* time was gone — linear and monochromatic; he had become tuned, he tells us,

> towards something else, a reality where the poem, the little book of Joyce, the reading and the women, had survived time . . . With panic, with the benediction of my companions, with guilt and joy, I had come from the orders of the day, a

deserter, from my possible career as a poet-professor, from literary strategies and prizes to be, into the reading of a poem.[13]

He returned here in the beginning, then, to the primary powers of reading, that arc where the language of experience meets the experience of language; a reader among his elements . . . "and I feed upon prime."[14]

As a writing from reading poetics, these derivations propose an openness, an open-heartedness, a letting in of admissible evidence — in the dark and of the light, an "influence." "Occult ethereal fluid," as my hermetic dictionary has it, "flowing from the stars to affect the fate of men." And let these stars, too, be those other lights, Blake's eternal Authors, or Pound's heroes, where "the study of literature is hero-worship." And Duncan would transform this more dutiful worship by the addition of affection, so that his poetics, now, would include eros in the function of the reader/writer dynamics — a high sensuality and a receptive humility before the bearers of language. "Go, my songs, then," he says in his envoi at the end of the *Dante Etudes*, "in zealous / liberality, no longer mine, / but now the friendship of the / reader's heart and mind / divine."[15] As companions of the way, then, or as lovers on the way, readers and writers partner each other in a singular yet mutual engagement. "I derive all my forms," says Duncan, "and they come from adoration and falling in love with poets."[16]

This reading/writing nexus is a creative eros; the poet and reader in cohabitation are co-conspirators, co-creators, co-mmunal.

The poet and the reader, who, if he is intent in reading becomes a new poet of the poem, come to write or to read in order to participate through the work in a consciousness that moves freely in time and space and can entertain reality upon reality.[17]

One opens a book as the world rushes in. "Books," Duncan says,

are real and also imagined, and they must be included if we would draw upon all the life we have lived; life, a dream or stage on which we act, is also larger than the life we have lived, for its reality is extended in all the poets we have read.[18]

[1989]

Notes

1. *The H.D. Book*, Part II, Nights and Days, Chapter 4, in *Caterpillar* 7, p. 28. Note: at the time this piece was written, *The H.D. Book* was only available in parts, published in various small magazines (often copied and handed down by poet to poet), and in a so-called pirate edition, found online. It is now available in an authoritative version: Robert Duncan, *The H.D. Book*, ed. Michael Boughn and Victor Coleman, University of California Press, 2011.

2. "A Footnote" to "Returning to Les Chimeres of Gérard de Nerval," *Audit*, Vol. IV, No. 3, p. 49.

3. "On Pound and Williams," *American Poetry*, Vol. 6, No.1, p. 34.

4. "Rites of Participation," *The H.D. Book*, Part I, Chapter 6.

5. "The Adventure of Whitman's Line," *Fictive Certainties*, New Directions, 1985, p. 199.

6. "A Footnote."

7. "Man's Fulfillment in Order and Strife," *Fictive Certainties*, p. 113.

8. "Beginnings," *The H.D. Book*, Part I, Chapter 1.

9. "The Adventure of Whitman's Line," *Fictive Certainties*, p. 198.

10. *Bending the Bow*, New Directions, 1968, p. ix.

11. "Changing Perspectives in Reading Whitman," *The Artistic Legacy of Walt Whitman*, ed. E. H. Miller, New York University Press, 1970, p. 100.

12. "A preface" in *MAPS* No. 6, p. 6.

13. "Beginnings."

14. "Preface" to "Dante Etudes," *Ground Work: Before the War*, New Directions, 1984, p. 94.

15. "Go, My Songs, Even As You Came to Me," *Ground Work: Before the War*, p. 122.

16. *"Robert Duncan: An Interview"* by George Bowering and Robert Hogg, A Beaver Kosmos Folio, 1969.

17. "Rites of Participation."

18. Ibid.

Among *way*

On Leslie Scalapino's way

One among many — not *the* — even though they converge on
one place or instant, their convergence makes them multiple:
ways. Our urgency, in fact, to be singular, discrete, Leslie Scalapino reveals as an impossible horror, something "viewed as not
subject to/change – that as irrelevant – but / which really occurs that way – as / conservative." We are, as her long poem *way*
insists over and over again, in "relation," and in our social body
dependent on each other. Her interruptive dashes refuse any
such dream of contained coherence as a sentence might argue,
and her language slants continually along the angular lines of
dependent or passive verb tenses, participles on the aside and
past perfects qualified by their simple pasts.

Along these ways our heads are turned by a ceaseless series
of accidental destructions, from which we turn in longing to
literally "not see," but toward which Scalapino determinately
focuses our gaze, "struggling – so that one wouldn't / be inter-
preted from the setting – when / that is continual." Muggings,
shootings, homeless dying in the street, bullying cops, happening around us, of us, and in us, demand a focus whose sympathy is in the complexity of the lens, not just the affective sentiment (though "it's physical – so it is sentiment"). And since
memory and desire also qualify events, one needs a constantly
shifting frame which aims at multiple exteriors and interiors,
superimposed on each other. Scalapino's interrupted sentences
and truncated breathless first lines labor to nail experience, yet
remain astonished and willing before its complexities and com-
partmentalizations to let it go its several ways — perplexed but
dreaming of (desire!) causality ("throwing / themselves / away

/ throughout / a time / occurring / for / a reason"), a hunger for placement subsumed by the hunger for the multiple truths of memory and event.

The real urgency in a world, then, is to get *inside* "their view" before it's too late,

> the bums – the men – having
> died – from
> the weather — though their
> doing that, seeing things from their view when
> they were alive.

In *way* one participates among the relations of the "social struggle" — the author, dead "bums," a man in new wave attire, the "present president," a freighter unloading — as in the mystery of contiguities and simultaneities that constitute a nevertheless exact moment of world's life. Reading Scalapino, one cannot be sure where one is, but one can be sure one is there.

There is humility in this stance — this willingness to be broken apart — and fierce clarity. She is permitting herself — she is trying to — experience experience, rather than demand experience order itself along predesignated routes of perception. She is after

> the relation
> of
> what's
> done – and
> making
> it – in the
> life
> of people.

[1989]

Note

Leslie Scalapino, *way*, North Point Press, 1988.

The People's P***k

A Dialectical Tale

In the war of letters between Robert Duncan and Denise Levertov — the essential contention around poetry and politics, agenda and surrender, that marks both the evolution and devolution of their thirty-year correspondence — one might be easily persuaded to side with one or the other, to hunker down in position held by fierce idealism or sanctimony as it may be, and rest in that resolve as though the contention had been concluded. As an act of politics such determination might be persuasive; as a poetics it may be seen as preliminary if not suspicious, and against practice per se. The social forces that pressure the creative use of language have not yet given ground to the imagination; the agony of how to speak into, over, through, or from history is a compositional struggle engaged by each generation, each poet, each reader.

How do we claim forebears? How do the articulations of our heroes dramatize our own contentions? When is poetics, or how may it be, the third position in a dialectic? Any of us — students and teachers alike (and many of us are both) — participate *experientially* in esthetic dialogue as we claim affinities, derivations, literary genealogies based on friendships, personal communication, affection, or argument. The Duncan/Levertov correspondence distills both poetics and action into a high-minded critique of personal practice — it is mostly Denise's practice that is critiqued — and the wave of righteous intelligence animating Duncan's defense of the imagination is often hard to counter. The embrace of discovery, accident, Freudian shame or slip, wayward invention, chance; of surprise and contradiction, danger and tangent ("I can't help it, I'm a tangent queen!" a

151

brilliant, talkative friend once said to me) are so fundamental to postmodern procedure as to be almost unquestionable. And yet the Patriot Act impinges; the war in Iraq, 9/11, Palestine, abortion rights, AIDS: any confidence in esthetic solution must be provisional, unless none of these key inciters means anything to you. (I recently listened to an Argentine writer, who had been "disappeared," whose brother had been terminally disappeared, discuss her struggle to find the formal shape for a fictionalized memoir which might raise a response [and what kind of response do we seek?] greater than that offered by a litany of facts.) If we question the efficacy of Levertov's solutions — how was her poetry altered by her convictions and how do we measure the failure or success of those alterations? — her sense of urgency is hard to question. Duncan's grand collage, which includes worlds of destruction *and* instruction, is a bliss of a magus overview we might seek to attain as poets but fail to meet as nervous humans.

If Levertov came to see writing as an argumentative means to action, Duncan saw it as an already active mode, wherein contentions aren't argued or answered so much as rendered visible, as *made*. Both were profoundly communal writers, both teachers in the literal and general sense. How might a student of either or both — and how is a reader a student? — come to a synthesis mutually engaging? To honor positions taken with such vehemence one can offer vehement attention. To read their correspondence richly as if it mattered *now* is to argue with *oneself*. The following is a necessarily personal account in which *The Letters of Robert Duncan and Denise Levertov* are at risk.

***

As part of my literary biography, I often joke to those in the know that I'm the bastard son of Robert Duncan and Frank O'Hara, an heir to seemingly irreconcilable poetic territories: diction high and low; mythopoetic drama and breezy, urban rhythm; Esclarmonde de Foix in her holy fortress and Lana Turner in her turban; communal San Francisco and vigorous, imperial New York (I was born and raised as a child in Manhattan, have lived my adult life in S.F.). But the truth is I'm the lovechild of Denise Levertov and Robert Duncan. Each was my longtime poetic mentor, teacher, beloved friend, spiritual guide, and muse. For each I was apprentice, acolyte, amanuensis, confidant, communer, and fellow traveler.

From early 1969, when I met Denise, to Robert's death in 1988, they were the highest comrades of my poetic community; their work awakened me to the power and possibility of American poetry, and called me forward into my own imagination and practice. If our friendships swelled or faded as did their own, mastery notwithstanding, the work was resolute. Such graces of encounter are not casual. As in the familial paradigm (Robert died the same year as my father), individuation is the synthesis of deep obedience and disavowal: In the crisis of these poets' unfolding esthetic and political conflict my own writing was tested and proved — and still is.

***

In the spring of 1969 I was nearing the end of my undergraduate days at Berkeley, a tenure reaching from the close of the Free Speech Movement (in which my brother Isak, to whom Levertov's "Relearning the Alphabet" is dedicated,[1] was arrested) through vivid, multiple protests against the Viet Nam buildup, conscription, and university racism, along with various unnamed armed conflicts (my twenty-first birthday found me under curfew-driven house arrest as national guardsmen patrolled each civic corner; I remember the fact, but who can remember the reason why?) as well as through the Summer of Love, the great Human Be-in, the Fillmore, the Avalon, Hendrix, and Joplin; through, too, uncountable nights charting my own adventurous forlorn and ecstatic forays into gay life in the City; all seeming to culminate, then, in the epochal war-at-home known as the battle for People's Park. How can the spring of 1969 in Berkeley be registered without such coordinates, the *feel* of cultural seismology and the pressure of localized national events? So when Denise's poetry class answered the call to come work at People's Park, each of those historical ganglia was waving, charged, and for each of us, I think, symbolic action was fed by these cumulative empowerments and disempowerments.

It must have been a bright sunny day, that May 14 Denise describes in "Staying Alive,"[2] because I remember the sheen on the green as we rolled out great swaths of sod like a carpet to cover the ground of the park. The school quarter had been peppered with demonstrations and student strikes and we'd often, if I remember correctly, met off campus; that we should go together to work at the park was testimony to our support of Denise's political conviction as well as our belief that the common purposes of poetry made a place for voice in the space of action; "the personal is political" extended its alliterative syllogism to include "poetry." Denise describes scooping up debris to haul away to a dump and who could help imagining that a red wheelbarrow might have been involved?

That specific domestic conflict was galvanizing, and in a particularly San Francisco way the poetic community came alive to its civic urgency, and called together a resplendent literary gathering to raise money for the park. On Monday, June 2, the great California Hall was the site of an overflowing "Poetry Reading for the People's Park," with appearances by Levertov, Duncan, Brautigan, Ferlinghetti, Snyder, McClure, and others. The scene was raucous, celebratory, serious, committed, with overtones of literary history and an aura of cultural significance, fed by the political drama of the immediate weeks and orchestrated by Denise's role as MC.

What fate, I can almost hear Robert ask, was at work in bringing Denise to that role on that stage that night, where her uses of poetry and her use by poetry met their boundaries and overflowed? The chaotic (post-Beat?) impulses of the Bay Area cultural scene were different from those of the Movement that was framing her current practices, and her sober streak hardened in direct proportion to the gospel-like fervor, the shrieks and laughter, the carnal carnival of the gathered masses. As she felt the crowd inch beyond her control — beyond her intentions as if the poem itself refused to obey her projections — where she would bring it back to a political formulation exactly as the audience was riding its imagination — a face came over her face that was a borrowed face, a stern righteous visage that wasn't a poetic face yet was exactly what Robert saw or feared he saw as the face of her war poems.

As if on cue, up onto the stage from somewhere in the audience jumped an eight-foot pink felt penis, who grabbed the mike and announced to the crowd that he was "The People's Prick," bouncing around like a giant bunny on LSD. The audience roared their approval (the other operative syllogism extended "free all political prisoners" into "free love") — but not Denise. She was outraged. She was affronted. She knew better. She tried to take back control, hectoring the audience to behave with a puritan, if not Stalinist, regard that made it clear that Emma Goldman's revolution was not *her* revolution. But the *audience* was *not* hers. The Prick defied her, danced around her, as her sense of offence congealed and straightened her unbending spine into something far more disturbingly erect.

I no longer remember how events progressed after that, but for me the image of the clash between the embodied pleasure principle and the officer of the doctrinaire has stood precisely for the poetic trouble Robert envisioned when he cautioned Denise that her public poetic thinking was "a force that, coming on *strong*, sweeps away all the vital weaknesses of the living identity; the *soul* is sacrificed to the demotic persona that fires itself from spirit" [letter 409],[3] and, later, "The poet's role is not to oppose evil, but to imagine it. . . . Is it a disease of our generation that we offer symptoms and diagnoses of what we are in the place of imaginations and creations of what we are?" [Letter 452],[4] or, even at the very beginning of their correspondence, "The feeling of what is false for me is the evident *use* of language to persuade" [Letter 21].[5] And how, in the end, can we not be reminded of Duncan's Freudian complaint, which so enraged Denise, that read into the skinned-penises of "Life at War" "an effect and tone of disgusted sensuality."[6]

He would not be alone, here, in registering the break between Movement politics and the socio-political implications of cultural and personal exploration, which found their catalysts in the emerging Women's and Gay liberation movements — even if this insight did not succeed in liberating poetry from the rhetoricizing projections of those very countering insurgencies. Yet there my poetry fled, bounding into the communal arms of gay comrades, who fought both the male domination of the power brokers of the revolution and the homophobia and heterosexism that fed it. The rhetoric was heavy; the poems groaned under its weight. But if I'd understood the problem that lay within the People's Prick scenario, it went only so far as to resurrect (re-erect?) issues of pleasure — the life of Eros and the social registrations of its repression — from the peace movement's cemetery, but not yet entirely to question the poem's obedience to my instructions. The American people's red army may have been mutated, but if you read the poetry in my first book (and you needn't) you will find that I was frequently writing like a new pink officer of the doctrinaire.

The spring of People's Park marked the beginning, not the end, of my friendship with Denise. In fact, she had given me every sense of poetry's immediacy and magic; the California Hall reading was a small event in a large apprenticeship. We both moved east that summer, and stayed in proximity for years. The finesse of her poetic line — its rhythmic and perceptual discriminations — remains for me, with Creeley's, the definitive American investigative verse line (though the writing I *refer* to largely predates the war poems). The disciplinarian that seemed in evidence later was not so in evidence earlier; instead there was the most joyful, appreciative, wonder-seeking and wonder-giving person I'd yet met. This is the same writer Robert adored, a poet whose aural and visual access to a sensory world places her in the company of H.D. and Dickinson, of Colette and Virginia Woolf, a writer capable of an audible hush into which a melodic apprehension of experience is raised precisely into language.

I've found, in rereading letters, that sympathy to gay ideology as it was forming was not intuitive to her, though her sympathy to *me* was, and we discussed in person and through correspondence the arguments and articulations of gender construction and sexual liberation. She was frankly confused, and interested in being educated; from her few responses I must have offered my own (communally derived) convictions and cant about male domination and power. (A letter from 1972 has probing questions from her about homosocial theory, and naive ones about homoerotic formation and even wicked hairdressers.) We visited regularly, and spoke with great emotional intimacy, and each visit for me was a privileged occasion. By the time I moved to

San Francisco in the summer of 1974 we'd been in less-frequent contact; a letter sent in 1975 shows we'd been out of touch for a while. It contains a reference to the idea of, and the seeds to, her poem "Writing to Aaron," which appeared in *Life in the Forest*,[7] and which raised a consonant pang in Robert — "And that's how we lost touch for so long" [Letter 472].[8] And when, in 1976, my first book was published, I sent it to Denise with expectant pride. The irony of her response was bitter: "Some of your poems are too emphatically homosexual for me to identify with, as you surely realize," she wrote.

> When I seem to detect a note of propaganda it turns me off completely. But when you are simply writing poetry and transcending opinion then I can respond. This may sound inconsistent from one who has written 'political' poetry, but I believe my political concerns to be less parochial in theme.[9]

Her analysis of dogma infecting my poetry per se could have come right from Robert's critique of her own writing, though the second part was hers alone, and the wound it opened between us was never really healed. She was telling me, in fact, that it wasn't a poetic argument that most mattered to her: the argument was political and revolved around the supremacy of her own ideology. Parochial! If I (thought I) was busy tying up racism, misogyny, homophobia, and warmongering into a unified theory of oppression, her authoritarianism split the weave, and unraveled me where I was most in need of support, where my own personal sense of oppression was, in fact, most tenderly situated. This double face of her response had the power of revelation: of a true homophobia in her nature ("too emphatically homosexual") that called forth the same stern disapproving persona who so vehemently opposed The People's Prick.

***

It occurs to me now that Denise's ruffled recalcitrance may have hidden the fact that I had recently met and formed a friendship with Robert Duncan. I must have told her, and she must have felt in a paranoid way — as she certainly did later — that this new association implied a censure and maybe even a kind of gay alliance.

I'd met Robert on a Market Street trolley in 1975, capping an imaginative sequence begun earlier in the week. I'd had a dream in which a rainbow loop of light appeared to me on a cliff top, raising such howling winds that I was nearly driven over. A hand appeared from a nearing car to steady me, and bring me safely into the presence of the enormous, pulsating light. I awoke and named that light "Jehovah," and wrote a poem that seemed to me, then, all my own, with the sense of finding my true way into poetry for the first time. The next day, in a bookstore, I chanced upon *The Opening of the Field*, and opened directly to the poem "A Natural Doctrine" in which a Rabbi Aaron of Bagdad "came upon the Name of God and achieved a pure rapture." "But it was for a clearing of the sky . . . my thought cried," writes Robert, and, "the actual language is written in rainbows."[10] Just a few days later I spied him on the bus, introduced myself, recounted in the most astonished way the correspondences between my dream and the poem, flush with the magic of circumstance, synchronicity, or fate. I remember distinctly that Robert was unimpressed by the linkage, as if this foretelling were a matter of course, utterly quotidian. But he was just enough impressed with me to invite me come to visit him, which I soon did.

I brought with me my first chapbook publication, and read it aloud;[11] Robert's response was gleeful and warm. The piece united themes of ritual transvestism, gender deconstruction, and plain ol' drag, and even by that time the writing was willing to be "fabulous" — to test the bounds of content permission and diction — in a way that was directly related to my reading of Duncan. His response, and our connection, I would say, was not based on some perceived or evident gay fraternal alliance but rather on this common understanding (my understanding under the wing of his) that the writing would be permitted to go where it needed to go, unabashed. It could never be "too emphatically homosexual" only because it could never be "too" *anything* in terms of limit or censure. This revelatory position in relation to permission was the foundation of my understanding of Robert's poetics, the key to his cosmic orchestrations and orchestral modulations — and remains so.

***

For me, from then, the conflict was resolutely resolved in terms of the poem's form being isometric with its (emerging) content, and a belief that when the poem is infected by the right-thinking politics which is dogma — replacing flexible attention with inflexible intention — it dies on the vine. Though Robert knew of my friendship with Denise, and I remember early on his addressing the issue in terms that were insufficiently clear to me so I may only have nodded sheepish assent, it was not really a subject of our conversation. By the 1980s it was clear that Denise was staying away from San Francisco, possibly so as not to have to contend directly with Robert. (A letter from 1980 states "I just can't take that SF scene — was there in secret last summer & don't dig it.")[12]

But then something came into view that challenged *my* political will, that threatened to deliver the politic back into the poetic in a way unmatched in the previous fifteen years: AIDS. By the late 1980s AIDS had ravaged San Francisco, seizing the territory of both action and imagination, and how to write about or into AIDS became, for me, an unavoidable confrontation, and challenged explorative composition with its insistence of thematic content. Advocacy, action, information were demanded; the very nature of the epidemic spewed information and viral activity. At a loss as to how to meet this troubling matter in poetry without resorting to didacticism, I turned to prose to help me carry the more direct addresses — the portraiture and narrative of events — that were consonant with my experience, built largely around the struggles and insights of friends, of "comrades," I want to say, "returning to the rhetoric of an early mode."[13]

But when I finally found the means to write complexly about AIDS through poetry it was not dogmatic and was not presumptuously moralizing; the piece ("Human Immune") carried elegiac weight through a *formal* ideology, built on an epidemiological model: each stanza grew by design larger than the previous, subsumed it, so that without realizing it the reader was brought *inside* the epidemic, as if surrounded by the virus. And I spoke not from my own first person, but from a range of subject/object, singular, and plural points of view to suggest the invariability of risk and loss. I spoke, in fact, as just such a People's Prick who in an earlier era jumped onstage to announce the pleasure principle, but here the pleasure was inextricably conjoined with pain: "I squirted them with kisses. On his back at the edge of the couch to die of pleasure . . ."[14] To say the words that couldn't be said to address the content that had to be spoken — the sacramental profane — with a phallic imperative, to "penetrate into their historian's hearts and foist upon the reader authenticity of the marvels."

The oracle, whose exact charge was to speak into the unspeakable, had stepped forward and demanded ground. "I want that energy while speaking, place yourselves close by me, excessive behavior swell discourse in proportion." Since the disease itself was not a moral occasion, the poem needed to voice *not-myself* arising from *not-my-moral-circumstance*, and would range in accordance with the full multiphasic ceremony of public and secret acts. The permission I needed to write the poem could not have come from hounding the penetrating organ off the stage.

The test and retest of esthetics informed by convictions, the vision of art's purposes and possibilities in relation to or *as* action, remain the core processes enacted by — and *engendered* by — the Duncan/Levertov correspondence. If sympathy to Robert's poetics excited my own writing, the passionate advocacy and determination to speak into *un*necessary silence I'll trace to both mentors — and the poetics of their contention is dialectically *in* me. I've only ever counted such dual inheritance as one of extraordinary luck: their immediate graces mine to learn from, their tensions played out in the parameters of my work. The spiraling conversation is acute: "A mind hovering ecstatic / above a mouth in which the heart rises,"[15] writes Robert, and Denise will answer, "The poem ascends."[16]

[2003]

Notes

1. Denise Levertov, *Relearning the Alphabet*, New Directions, 1970, p. 110.

2. Denise Levertov, *To Stay Alive*, New Directions, 1971, pp. 43, 44.

3. Robert J. Bertholf and Albert Gelpi, eds., *The Letters of Robert Duncan and Denise Levertov*, Stanford University Press, 2004, p. 607.

4. Ibid., p. 669.

5. Ibid., p. 34.

6. Ibid., p. 749.

7. Denise Levertov, *Life in the Forest*, New Directions, 1978, p. 5.

8. Bertholf and Gelpi, p. 714.

9. Unpublished personal correspondence, January 26, 1977.

10. Robert Duncan, *The Opening of the Field*, Grove Press, 1960, p. 81.

11. Aaron Shurin, *Woman on Fire*, Rose Deeprose Press, 1975.

12. Unpublished personal correspondence, July 13, 1980.

13. Robert Duncan, *Roots and Branches*, Charles Scribner's Sons, 1964, p. 89.

14. Aaron Shurin, *Unbound*, Sun & Moon, 1997, p. 54.

15. Robert Duncan, "Circulations of the Song," *Ground Work: Before the War*, New Directions, 1984, p. 168.

16. Denise Levertov, *The Jacob's Ladder*, New Directions, 1961, p. 37.

IV.

Inhabiting Both Sides

Aaron Shurin's Correspondences

An Interview with Lily Iona MacKenzie

LILY IONA MACKENZIE: I want to start with the essay "Narrativity" that you published in 1990 and this particular quote:

> I'm interested in the utilization of both poetic and narrative tensions: the flagrant surfaces of lyric, the sweet dream of storied events, the terror of ellipsis, the audacity of disloca-tion, the irreversible solidity of the past tense, the incarnate lure of pronouns, the refractability of pronouns, the simul-taneity of times, the weights and balances of sentences. I'm interested in lyric's authenticity of demonstration and narra-tive's drama of integration; lyric, whose operation is display, and narrative, whose method is seduction.

What was the context for this piece on narrativity?

AARON SHURIN: It was first given as a talk at a place called the Painted Bride in Philadelphia. Later, when Doug Messerli from Sun & Moon Press was starting a chapbook series called Twenty Pages, this was one of the first chapbooks he put out. (It's also, now, online and also appeared in *Biting the Error*, an anthology of new narrative theory.)

MACKENZIE: What prompted you to talk about this particular subject?

SHURIN: I had already started writing prose poems, so the dynamic intersection of prose and poetry that is a prose poem was very much on my mind. Also, what the prose poem gathered from prose, particularly how to use narrative and how to incorporate narrative into a poetic form and structure, interested me.

The new narrative writers that I was very close to were simultaneously engaged in articulating a new narrative theory around personal experience.

MACKENZIE: Who were some of those poets?

SHURIN: They were in general prose writers rather than poets. Bob Glück especially. Kevin Killian, Dodie Bellamy, and others. I've been very close to Bob: He and I pretty much began publishing together in the early gay press and have been colleagues and confrères since. I've been enormously close to his writing and influenced by it. As I got more housed in the prose poem, I got more interested in narrative *per se*. *Narrativity* talks about Kevin and it talks about Bob. It talks about a variety of narrative strategies related to poetry or experimental prose — (Bob, Kevin, Dodie, and Bruce Boone were mostly prose writers, but they really "lived" in the poets' community) — and of my interest in conflating narrative and lyric components. A writing invested in subjectivity and person and event, but also in rhetoric and sound and measure and phonemic density and the opacity of language. It seemed to me — in the dialogue that was kicked off by language poetry — one was challenged to be on one side or the other, one side of "representation" or the other. I never wanted to surrender either side, so I tried to articulate what was my organic pursuit anyway — the conflation of two modes: poetic surface, let's say, and narrative depth. In my own intellectual and creative life, anytime there's a binary system, I'm drawn to inhabit both sides.

MACKENZIE: Yes!

SHURIN: That would be true of gender, too, which is part of what I talk about in *Narrativity*: maneuvering through gender position so that a speaker becomes a kind of malleable or faceted or unlocated subject on the gender spectrum.

MACKENZIE: Many of your poems move fluidly among gender. At times you're clearly inhabiting the female point of view. Other times it sounds like a male perspective.

SHURIN: Right.

MACKENZIE: But many seem to be persona poems.

SHURIN: I'd say they're just shy of persona. I would say person rather than persona. They're constructed by the voice or pronoun of the indicated speaker rather than by some mask of a person or identity. They're less than a persona because they're only there as far as the speaking subject.

MACKENZIE: In that particular poem.

SHURIN: In that instance, yes.

MACKENZIE: I'm curious about something that's been said about gay poetry in general, especially for poets who are more innovative in their work. It's suggested that the layering of texts that partially conceals the writer's identity parallels the way gay identity often must be concealed and glimpsed through layers. Do you think being gay affects your choice of poetics, and do you think there's a gay poet's sensibility that's different say from a heterosexual poet's?

SHURIN: That's an ongoing question of shifting relevance, and part of that has to do with the historical development of society and culture. There was definitely a point where one needed to claim it, claim the experience, claim the identity, and even claim the words — flaming faggots and such, or *Fag Rag*, the radical journal, or later *Queer Nation.* I think all those things were crucial, and I certainly participated in them. I've never masked the sexuality in my poems unless I was interested in creating a specific non-homosexual experience (which I do all the time), but that's different from masking. Gay material has always been forthright in my poetry. But I think as time goes on, the label "gay poetry" may become less informing rather than more informing. It begins to limit the context in which my work may be read or approached. I'm not sure now it's a particularly useful way of describing my poetry in any complex way. I think it can be included as part of the picture, and I would never negate its value as part of the picture. But there are so many other poetic and aesthetic components to my writing, as well as socio/cultural/historical valences, that to call it gay poetry doesn't find its dimension at this point. But it's not *not.*

MACKENZIE: Okay.

SHURIN: It's also.

MACKENZIE: It's also. I like that.

SHURIN: As to gay sensibility: I think it's a still-open debate. Unquestionably in the community there are traditions, and one learns from them and participates in them, and maybe there are socio/cultural alignments that find literary expression or equivalences, much like gender: expressiveness, flamboyance, sensuality, shamelessness, abjection . . . but none of these are limited to gay men, and of course not all gay writers are flamboyant or shameless . . .

MACKENZIE: I want to return to your choice of the prose poem and what led you to that form because your earlier work seemed more traditionally lyric poetry. Why did you make that shift?

SHURIN: I had been mesmerized by the line break, which I came to think of as the main focus, if not obsession, of the generation-plus that preceded me, the generation probably starting with Pound and Williams whose duty it was to discover a non-metrical line.

MACKENZIE: Right.

SHURIN: So a lot of their thinking about poetry — right up through Creeley and Levertov, Olson and even Duncan — the projective verse poets in particular — was about creating the line, the line as the focus of new a prosodic structure. They were my teachers, and so that was absorbing to me too. But after a while, it came to feel emptied out for me. I thought there are other things to obsess over in the poem, other urgencies and prosodic elements to be attended, and those earlier poets already did *that*. But more organically, the possibilities of prose poetry were emerging, I think, under the influence of Whitman. I started writing long lines, and the lines just got longer and longer until they started wrapping. In a way, once they started wrapping across the right margin say two times, they were hard to distinguish from prose. There wasn't any printing circumstance that was going to show a two foot-long line, let's say.

MACKENZIE: True.

SHURIN: So once they started wrapping, and as they got longer, I became interested in the kind of interior modulations possible within a long line: all the syntactic prose modulations, which include punctuation marks, the proposition of the beginning and end of a sentence, ellipses and interjection, subordinate clauses, etc. All of those possibilities became more various and interesting to me than the simple projective-based line break.

MACKENZIE: You use collage in many of your poems. For example, I was looking at *Into Distances,* and in the second stanza/ paragraph of the title poem, it reads, "She labored down the path barefoot . . . ." The poem's focus seems to be on a female character — the word grandmother comes up and so on — and it goes on for several pages. I'm wondering what moved you to write that particular poem. Where do you start?

SHURIN: There are two different ways of looking at it. What moved me to write that poem was all my experience and interest in the world. I don't think there was any given autobiographical moment or circumstance that one could equate with this pioneer panorama, which is part of the underpinning of that poem. Certainly part of it is the drama of landscape.

MACKENZIE: Yes.

SHURIN: That was one of the things that interested me in narrative, and prose theory, let's say: the use of landscape as a dramatic register. I had been reading a lot of H. Rider Haggard, the great, oddball Victorian novelist. Actually I wrote an essay about this for *Poetics Journal*. I came to see that if you look at modernism, from Joyce to Woolf to whomever, Robbe-Grillet, the impulse had been a withdrawal from descriptive locale, at least in part because the movies took it. If you want that, you go to see a movie in cinemascope, or now 3D or Imax. That kind of densely articulated landscape and action became the province of the movies. I liked that very much and wanted to incorporate the dramatic elements — panorama, foreground, and background — into my poetry. That is one of the underpinnings of a poem like "Into Distances." *Elsewhere* I think was collaged from H. Rider Haggard, if I remember correctly. Some of "Into Distances" came from Agnes Smedley. I don't know if you know her.

MACKENZIE: I don't.

SHURIN: She was a kind of post–Emma Goldman revolutionary, an American grass roots pioneer woman who also wound up participating in the Chinese revolution. She lived in China and may have marched in the long march. I don't remember exactly. I read several books of hers, but this was from *Daughter of Earth*, her autobiography. But that's neither here nor there. As in so much of the source material, it was simply what I was reading. Duncan has a beautiful quote where he says books are as real to me as persons or places. In a way, I took that on faith. My experience in books was primary, but it was also primary language experience. It was the site for me to find words to use, and I just found them often in what I was reading at present. But I would also have a disposition, yet I couldn't be reductive and tell you what the disposition to "Into Distances" was since it's such a strange and broadly cast poem. For other poems I would have had some disposition which might have just been I want to write something sexy, or I want to write something mysterious, or I want to write something light and lyrical. I would migrate to a Virginia Wolf book or a Colette book or a Raymond Chandler book where I knew an appropriate lexicon might be found. If I had a pastoral impulse, let's say, I wouldn't go to Raymond Chandler because I knew I wasn't going to find that language there. But I would go to Colette because I knew

I was going to find trees and flowers and sky. So I found the words to compose as I needed.

MACKENZIE: Your poetic dictionary.

SHURIN: My poetic dictionary, exactly.

MACKENZIE: When you're reading, then, are you underlining or highlighting things that grab you?

SHURIN: No. In the system I used for those books, and that would be starting with the later section of *A's Dream*, all of *Into Distances*, and all of *A Door*, I established rules for myself. Generally the rule was I could only move forward in the text. I couldn't go back. The thing I didn't want to do is search out what I needed because then it's just like normal composition. I wanted to find what I needed so I could reroute my compositional habits and my predictive combinations, let's say. Even predictive lexicon. So I had to be careful not to let myself look for what I wanted and rather let the poem find the words it needed. Almost always I would say I can only move forward in the text when choosing words. And there isn't a single word I can use that I don't see first. Any single word that appears in any of those poems arrives via the text. Every single word. 100%. Every "the," every "of," every "and," every "I," every "you."

MACKENZIE: What was the basis for that rule you made?

SHURIN: The basis was an extension of my original impulse toward constraint, which was to reroute the kind of suffocating tightness of my hand, which I came to feel was too bound, too controlling. And I wanted to reroute my poor brain so that I wasn't regurgitating the same kinds of experience habitually. I also didn't want to be limited by my own experience or my narrow knee-jerk interpretations or recall of my own experience. I was led into other, deeper reservoirs by finding language outside of my ready vocabulary.

MACKENZIE: Your collection, *The Paradise of Forms*, really is a paradise of forms. From what you've said, it sounds as if form is an important component of your approach to poetry.

SHURIN: Yeah. *The Graces* starts investigating prose poems and long lines. By the time of *A's Dream*, which was also collaged — even the non-prose poems were collaged, starting with I think "Artery," the first poem — all those poems use a certain collage methodology. By the end, the long poems that I was writing — not *Into Distances* but in *A Door* — some of the longer poems, especially the title poem and there was another one,

"Human Immune," used multiple simultaneous texts. I think the poem "A Door" used seven simultaneous texts. It was the most elaborate process. And then each text fed a stanza, and the stanzas were in rotation, and the stanzas also lengthened.

MACKENZIE: When you say in rotation, what do you mean?

SHURIN: Each stanza uses words derived from one book. The first seven stanzas are from the first seven books. Then stanzas eight through fourteen recapitulate the sequence. Stanza eight goes back to book one. Stanza nine goes back to book two. At the same time, they're expanding in length because I was interested in narrative depth and saturation, in exploring how to sustain narrative movement and intensity. So in its very free-form way, there were seven very slightly altered waves that were independent but fed the same poem, and the narrative tensions just got stronger as the stanzas got longer. It was 100% collaged, so at some point I had seven books open on my desk. I had created this kind of fabulous monster for myself. I loved working that way, but I think that was the end. It became a little unwieldy.

MACKENZIE: So when you are working in this way and you're using language that is coming from different sources, do you become conscious at some point of a thread that's developing?

SHURIN: Of course. The language is generative. And then you make or follow a way through. The great mystery of this process is that in the end it sounds like you. These poems sound like my poems. They have my voice in them. The mark of my head and my style and my poetic thought is all through them, which tells us something about language and authorship. And any poem, any language utterance, is about choice, so this is just rerouting the system of choice. But it really isn't any different. You choose the words (unless you're using a Cageian or a Mac Low-like pure-chance procedure.) But this isn't chance procedure, I'm choosing the words. There may be a lot of resistance put up by the procedure so that I can't over select them, because one of the rules is you have to move fairly fast. What's being sought is something other than your usual sense of combination or coherence.

MACKENZIE: It's a little like freewriting, only it's using other texts.

SHURIN: Yeah. And because it's so complex a process, it's not exactly free: it's a form. The intensity of composition is multiplied, I would say. So to go back to that question, sure, I always have a sense of what was informing the poem, though it

171

may be spontaneously developed. I just expanded my sense of what that structure could be, of what meaning could be.

MACKENZIE: Did this impulse toward form ever encourage you to try some of the traditional forms other than the sonnet, which you have done in *Involuntary Lyrics*.

SHURIN: I wasn't so interested in traditional forms. This was my version of a traditional form. I was interested in forms. I'm interested in the pressure of what form provides, but the traditional forms seemed of their period and emptied out. These other constraints were more interesting to me. When *Involuntary Lyrics* came along, it was, for me, a reduced procedure of using just the end words of Shakespeare's lines. But still it has the essence of the use of the form as a compositional aid to reroute the brain. In a way, the form helps to enact a combined left-brain and right-brain poetry: one side has to do with vision and what you see, and one side has to do with your language usage. In the case of the collage methodology used in *Involuntary Lyrics*, what I see or what is there is the end word of Shakespeare's sonnets. So in combining the right brain and the left brain emphases, or we could call it the right hand and the left hand, where one is fixed (the seen word) and the other is mutable (the rest of the line) — let's say language is a left-brain activity, but visual perception is a right-brain activity. If you're *seeing* text, if the language is arriving through visual recognition, you're rerouting the left-brain activity into the right-brain activity. So I felt this kind of holistic energization that permitted me an entry into another way of seeing. I wrote, in part, with my eye, with my eye in my hand!

MACKENZIE: And also you reinvented the sonnet in certain ways.

SHURIN: In certain ways, but I tend to say those aren't sonnets. I've had an argument with a poet who has insisted because they are fourteen lines, they are sonnets and that's the determining nature of the sonnet. I don't think that. *Involuntary Lyrics* isn't written in what I call sonnet mind when I teach the prosody course, which I believe is the defining element of the sonnet. I'd sooner think a poem with eleven lines and sonnet mind could be a sonnet rather than a non-sonnet-minded poem of fourteen lines.

MACKENZIE: I get it.

SHURIN: So they derived from sonnets, or they were in correspondence with sonnets, but I don't think of them as sonnets.

MACKENZIE: Except I was looking at them as a new form of sonnet.

SHURIN: Yes, they could be, though I wasn't thinking of sonnets. That's all I'm saying. They don't have turns. On the other hand I would say at various points — rather more because of Shakespeare than because of sonnet — there is a kind of rhetoric and a syntax that's sonnet like, at least in terms of being Elizabethan.

MACKENZIE: Yes, a voice comes through in some of them that sounds like the bard speaking.

SHURIN: Right. That was because I was using all of the end words. Well the end words are the rhyme words. They are a kind of easy storehouse, and also show what's acceptable to the Elizabethan ear. Words like love and time come up a lot, which aren't so easy to use in contemporary circumstance in the same way. So when time comes up and when love comes up, it's an abstracted lexicon that we might normally shun. I couldn't because they were there; they were the end rhymes; that was the rule. I think part of that spirit of the historical language, and the rhetoric associated with the language, gives the poems at points an elevated tone, which to our ear is a little reminiscent of sonnets — which I'm delighted with.

MACKENZIE: Was there a lot of collage as well in *Involuntary Lyrics*? It didn't feel like it.

SHURIN: None. Just the end words.

MACKENZIE: The poems seem to express more of your own day-to-day concerns or interests.

SHURIN: That was part of the project. I wanted the quotidian to be part of the material. I wanted there to be high and low. I wanted to cast a wide net. And I wanted there to be the high-minded sentiment that some of the sonnets express. I also wanted quotidian life to counter the high-mindedness. I think *Involuntary Lyrics* is marked by these wide shifting tonalities of rhetoric and diction.

MACKENZIE: Yes, it's rich in variety and shape. It's a wonderful text for teaching poetry.

SHURIN: Thanks. I've always thought it would be. Long lines and short lines . . . .

MACKENZIE: Exactly. And some of the single words in columns and how they all hook up in unusual ways. Some poems start as if the reader is walking into the middle of something, and others start more formally. To change direction for a moment, where does *King of Shadows* fit in to the chronology of books you've published?

SHURIN: *King of Shadows* came after *Involuntary Lyrics.* Then there
was a two-year period of relaxation, and mostly that's because I
wrote *Involuntary Lyrics'* 154 poems in a year and a half.

MACKENZIE: Intense!

SHURIN: It was quite a compressed experience. What I kept saying
to myself afterward is I don't feel depleted, I feel completed.

MACKENZIE: Wonderful.

SHURIN: I felt like I had completed the gesture and then
completed this kind of return to the line. The book was really
a crazed reinvestigation of what that torque of a line break can
be. And that line-break torque can just about take your head
off in *Involuntary Lyrics.* I think that was one of the primary
investigations I undertook and played with.

MACKENZIE: Talk a little more about what you learned about the
line and line breaks from doing *Involuntary Lyrics.*

SHURIN: Well, the learning was in the sense of performing rather
than something you take away: something you enact (though
I did learn to be more fearless.) There were a bunch of things
I was interested in prosodically in *Involuntary Lyrics.* One was
what the torque of the line could be and how syntax might
be manipulated or creatively employed in the service of that
torque, which is engendered by the set word that is ending
the line. That word is likely to be enjambed in the middle of a
perception; otherwise it would be all end-stops. So how do you
go across it; what do you do with this word that's sitting there
in some way at the end but also in the middle? I found that a
kind of jumpy syntax could absorb the radical shifts from line
to line these set words demanded. So that was one thing. Also,
these were all rhyme words, so one of the things I wanted to
investigate was how to use the rhymes without them being sing-
songy.

MACKENZIE: Right.

SHURIN: Then it really would have been just a sonnet, since these
were all rhyming words. So I found out how to take them out
of order. That was the impulse behind making long lines and
short lines in the same poem because I wanted to see how a
measure of eight accents versus a measure of two accents, say,
with a rhyme at the end of each, would affect the rhyme. How
much your ear would hear it or not. In general the idea was
to not hear it — to let the rhyme be there but to not hear it.
So *Involuntary Lyrics,* both via kind of very fluid syntax and
variation of line length, tries to find a way of permitting but

not over inscribing the rhymes that are sent there from the Shakespeare poems.

MACKENZIE: Has that experience made you want to do more with the traditional line?

SHURIN: Actually, no. I think that experience made me feel completed in relation to the line. Then for five years I wrote pure prose, which was *King of Shadows*. And now I've just completed *Citizen*, which is a return to prose poems.

MACKENZIE: What was the shift like for you from writing "poetry" to writing *King of Shadows*, which is mainly "prose"?

SHURIN: To me it is definitely prose, and not even prose poems. It's different than prose poems; it's much more narrative. It's also essayistic, discursive, and dramatic: it has scene. As well as complex language and sentence structure . . .

MACKENZIE: And the lyricism . . . .

SHURIN: And the lyricism.

MACKENZIE: I think *King of Shadows* has very lyrical prose.

SHURIN: Yeah, that's always part of my writing and what I'm interested in. I wrote something like this prose in *Unbound*. I knew *King* was a more mature circumstance, and it was going to be a larger gesture. It was incredibly difficult. I felt I had to teach myself how to write prose, invent the prose I needed to write.

MACKENZIE: What made it so difficult?

SHURIN: One, the territory was new. In *Involuntary Lyrics*, I was in verse, in lines, which I knew so well, and in a kind of poetry which I knew so well. It was a lark. I knew exactly what I wanted to do in *Involuntary Lyrics*. It was all familiar. It was new in the sense of a new project, but I know how to write poetry. But in *King of Shadows*, I even have dialogue. The idea of writing dialogue was just appalling to me.

MACKENZIE: Why?

SHURIN: Because I don't know how to do it. I have no experience, and it's a very different beast. Very different. What's the negotiation between the formal registers of how you write people's speech and how they actually talk? How does it serve a narrative structure? Then all the shifts in point of view and description and action. It required all of the complex aspects of my prose poetry that combined lyrical and dramatic texture, but it was also "real," nonfiction. The one rule that was operative in writing the pieces in *King of Shadows* was I wanted narrative to carry the day, but I also wanted to be able to write about anything. So what I thought was that not even a thought took place without being located in a body or person in place and time. There would be no thought in this book unless a person in a particular circumstance was thinking it. That became the model for the narrative. Even if I thought "Oh, I want to write about this garden . . ." I can't just write about this garden. I can write about being in the garden in relation to the garden and what I'm thinking about the garden as I'm in the garden. But if I'm home thinking about it, then I have to be in my house, in my home, in a time thinking about the garden. So everything was going to be housed inside of narrative coordinates of time and place and person. That was very different than the kinds of tensions poetry sustains.

MACKENZIE: Was it difficult to focus so much on your own personal history?

SHURIN: No, that wasn't difficult at all. In fact it's a common thing that people have said to me: Oh, you're so brave! Or how does it feel revealing all this stuff about yourself? My answer is it didn't feel weird at all. What would I want to do? Hide myself? The impulse is toward discovery of meaning, including the discovery of oneself. So there is no act that shame will try to cover — and this is very much under the tutelage of Duncan. There is no shame. There is just experience. And anyway, I don't presume that I'm the only poor little fool who had these experiences. So I have no shame, no compunction. Nor do I feel that I am revealing myself in any particular way, though other people feel that. I just feel this is experience and I'm interested in it. Let's find out what it was. I remember feeling such and such and I remember I did this or that. And these experiences all led to making a mature, interested human. I've made it to a pretty ripe place, so there's no reason to feel I need to censor any part. Personal history is just another history.

MACKENZIE: That's great.

SHURIN: That part was all quite easy to do. I did it with relish actually. I met myself in new ways. One of the things I did learn as I was writing *King of Shadows* is that the narrator as fool is a much more approachable figure, a more sympathetic figure, than the narrator as sovereign, let's say.

MACKENZIE: In a way that goes back to when you played Puck instead of Oberon in a high school performance of *A Midsummer Night's Dream*. From what I understand, your own impulses as a poet also started to stir then.

SHURIN: Yeah, I think they did. There are those few lines in *King of Shadows* where I talk about putting on the mask that would come to be my own true face. Actually, I have a lot of Oberon in me, but if you look at me, it's Puck who I am really. I don't know if that still equates to the fool, but in any event. . . .

MACKENZIE: But I think the fool and Puck are a wonderful conflation. I don't think they're mutually exclusive at all.

SHURIN: Right.

MACKENZIE: I think they're in harness.

SHURIN: Right. There's a fool in the *Commedia dell'arte* sense, which is quite different, or the wise fool.

MACKENZIE: And the fool in the Tarot that steps off the cliff, but it's that adventure spirit, that willingness to open oneself up to new experiences and not shut oneself down.

SHURIN: Yeah. As I was writing *King of Shadows* that was one of the main things I learned in constructing the identity of this person who stands for me. After all, it's not me; it's writing. But in all these autobiographical pieces there's this figure, a first person who is standing for me. I found that I had to place that figure, had to feel what the tenor of his point of view would be. I think I discovered a levity in relation to it, the poor fool in a tender sense, and it helped me distance myself, and find some humility in relation to the density of my experience. It helped me forgive myself, and understand myself better. But that was part of a long process — figuring out all these things that are part of prose that I'm not worried about in poetry where the pronouns are shifting, and the identities are shifting, and it's me or it's not me, or there is no "me."

MACKENZIE: What started you off on your most recent collection, *Citizen?*

SHURIN: The poems in *Citizen* were born in a panel presentation at the SF MOMA on the sculptor Martin Puryear, who was having a show there. We were asked to respond to Puryear's work. I took the invitation not as a critical occasion but really a moment to enact a work in relation to his sculpture. I felt I was being asked to write poetry. I had no idea what I would do or what mode or anything since I had just come out of *King of Shadows* and I hadn't written poetry for five years. So I went to the Puryear show with my little notebook and, spontaneously, as I was looking at the extraordinary and beautiful work, as I read the little museum tags, those descriptive panels, I decided to jot down words that named the materials he used — cedar or wagon or yellow or twine. That was the available lexicon. I went down and grabbed something to eat in the museum café and opened my notebook. Before I could say boo, I had written the words down in a loose grid in my notebook. I started writing, and every so often worked in one of the words from the grid that I had found on the Puryear tags. Soon enough, I had written a poem. I think my feeling was, well, my response to Puryear is to use the same materials but in poetry. But my version of the same materials was the words that were naming his materials. So I could say I did a Puryear sculpture using what he used, cedar and twine and wood and wagon, etc. You'll see in the first poem of *Citizen*, "an empty wagon flares on a hillside." I believe I wrote three poems for that occasion, all using those little grids. I went back and wrote down another set of words, and I thought that's interesting. It does some of what I'm interested in doing, which is to say it has a structural constraint, so it helps me kick out the tightness but not be so obsessive as in the 100% collages of *A Door.*

MACKENZIE: Right.

SHURIN: And as part of my presentation at the museum, I put together my one and only power point presentation where I took a picture of my notebook, the grid of the words, and I showed people the poem. And then I showed people the poem with the words derived from Puryear in bold face so they could see the structure. That then became the model. The book doesn't say, these poems were written with a grid. It's like saying they were written with a ballpoint or a fountain pen. Or they were typed or they were written at home or they were written outside. It's just a compositional aid of interest to people who are interested in compositional strategies. So all of *Citizen* was written in that way. They're all prose poems. But another thing relevant to *Citizen* is I was traveling a lot. I'm interested in place anyway, and there's a lot of place, a lot of different places, coming into the poems in *Citizen*. That's partly why the title is that. It's very saturated with the coordinates of the world, even when they are imaginary constructions and not autobiographical constructions. The work has a very permeable relation to the world of time and space.

MACKENZIE: And there's a lot of collage in these poems too?

SHURIN: No, only those little grids, which is usually somewhere between fifteen and twenty words. The poem could be a page or it could be half a page. Usually I try to use all the words, but I don't go crazy over it if they don't quite fit.

MACKENZIE: They'll go in the next one!

SHURIN: Yes, they do. There are a bunch of formal elements in *Citizen*, and one is that there are motifs that thread the book. There are five or six different repeated and modulated motifs that are like unifying threads that go throughout the poems. Some are repeated phrases. Some are repeated narrative tropes like "Once I was." Some are rhetorical structures. Repetition. There are about half a dozen different ones that appear any number of times throughout the book that unify it as something other than just a random collection.

MACKENZIE: When you're revising your work, do you have any particular revision process that you go through? Is it different with every poem, with every collection?

SHURIN: I don't have any process. It's just a matter of getting it right.

MACKENZIE: What would getting it right mean for you?

SHURIN: Getting it right would be the exact shade of any phrase that is both sonically and perceptually coherent on its own and in relation to the other parts of the poem. So something might have an extra beat, or something might have a shade of meaning slightly off than what I want in the set of correspondences that make up the poem. Or it may be too wordy or not wordy enough.

MACKENZIE: Do you read the poems aloud?

SHURIN: Always. That's the final register. It's not a completed poem until it meets the oral and auditory test.

MACKENZIE: I hear in your work a lot of music in how you use punctuation. You're also sensitive to the sounds of words, how they work together. Has music been important to you at all?

SHURIN: My poetry seeks to be music, so there's no kind of referential aspect. Music is as important to me as to most people, but the music of language, absolutely and always. The first poems that really marked my interest in poetry were the kind of rhyming narrative ballads of American poetry: "Casey at the Bat" and "Face upon the Barroom Floor," which I discovered as an adolescent and instantly memorized for no reason or occasion except I wanted to memorize the poems. If you're memorizing, especially if it's a metered rhymed poem, then you're inhabiting auditory structure. So that was the first thing that really articulated my interest in poetry. Then when I was seventeen and played Shakespeare and came to the great Oberon sequence, "I know a bank where the wild thyme blows." It was an experience of phonemic play that had immense authority for me and posed this kind of unity of semantic and phonemic density together that really would be my model for what poetry could be. For me, a poet's ear is the defining quality. A poet can be smart, can use kick-ass procedures, but if I don't sense a poet's ear, I cannot sustain an interest in the poem.

MACKENZIE: Are there contemporary poets you read whose work fits your criteria?

SHURIN: Any work that I go to has to have that quality.

MACKENZIE: Are there poets writing now that you look to for inspiration?

SHURIN: Sure. Michael Palmer is a great instance of a poet who has a lyric ear and a beautifully skeptical mind, which is to say the beauty of his poetry is that it retains lyric integrity while fulfilling a skepticism about lyric possibility. It both gives and takes away. It performs a deep suspicion of language and the whole structure of language meaning while at the same time enacting lyrical meaning in all its glory.

MACKENZIE: I understand that you read Proust. Does he inspire you in certain ways when you write?

SHURIN: Proust is one of the great lodestars for me, certainly as I began writing more prose, and I think the prose of *King of Shadows* bled over into prose poems in *Citizen*. Proust is the great genius of prose as far as I'm concerned. Your sense of literature and the possibilities of literature will be altered if you read Proust carefully, the whole thing.

MACKENZIE: Why do you think that is?

SHURIN: It's a monumental reinvention of the capacity of prose, both at a macroscopic level and at a microscopic level: the transcendental almost hallucinogenic vision combined with the scalpel-like Balzacian view of social structure, and the psychological Freudian-like unmasking of personal intention, behavior, and gesture. So many through lines of such intensity and integrity and maximalization are coexistent in Proust. To me it's a feast of full potential and has made me more fearless in pursuit of my own maximalism.

[2012]

Printed and bound by CPI Group (UK) Ltd, Croydon, CR0 4YY

09/06/2025

14686141-0001